AF352258

GOD AND YOUR FAMILY

DEVOTIONS FOR FAMILIES WITH YOUNG CHILDREN

BY LOIS VOGEL

CONCORDIA PUBLISHING HOUSE

SAINT LOUIS

CONCORDIA PUBLISHING HOUSE, ST. LOUIS, MISSOURI

COPYRIGHT 1963 BY CONCORDIA PUBLISHING HOUSE

Library of Congress Catalog Card No. 63-19961

ISBN 0-570-03128-1

7 8 9 10 11 12 13 14 15 16 CB 89 88 87 86 85 84 83 82 81 80

MANUFACTURED IN THE UNITED STATES OF AMERICA

Let's Have a Word Together

We have something in common. You and I both have families with small children. But we share more than similar families; we share the joy of knowing Jesus Christ as our Savior and Lord. These two similarities have brought about this book.

It is a real blessing having young children in our homes. They give us so many moments of happiness. They bring a touch of humor many times with their unusual attempts to show they are growing up. All too soon the years will slip away, and these little ones will have left our side. We don't want to waste even one precious moment with them.

We do find joy in our young ones, and part of this joy is the privilege of leading them to God. It is a thrilling experience to be able to show a child God's love in sending Jesus as his Savior.

Leading our children to the Lord is accomplished only with frequent use of God's Word. But I'll be the first to admit that devotions with young children are not always a quiet and serene time. More than once we have had to retrieve the youngest member of the family from under the table. Heads bowed devotedly have often freed little hands to do some mischief.

To help give everyone a chance to settle down, the devotions in this book begin with the family talking about things they have experienced. Several devotions use objects such as a flashlight or a burned-out light bulb. They help get the attention of even the smallest member of the family. They might spark a little curiosity in what is going to follow.

In the "Listening Together" section you will meet the Brown family. The four children are Bobby, 8; Betty, 7; Jimmy, 5; and Janey, 3. This isn't a perfect family. But the Browns do love their God and are thankful for His love in Jesus. Father and Mother Brown use God's Word to help

their children with the problems that come up in any Christian home.

Devotions with small children would not be complete without giving them a chance to say something. In the "Talking Together" section the children have an opportunity to express what they feel. You might even want to go beyond the questions that are suggested.

You will close your time of talking together by "Praying Together." A prayer is suggested for each devotion. Gradually through the book you will be encouraged to let the members of the family approach God themselves. You will find that even the smallest child enjoys this privilege of talking with God himself.

As you spend more time with God's Word and find yourself drawn closer to God, you will also find the members of the family drawn closer together.

May God richly bless you and your family as you spend a few moments each day together with God.

LOIS VOGEL

The Way to Heaven

I am the Way. John 14:6

BEGINNING TOGETHER. *Perhaps one of the children has at some time been lost or become separated from Mother in a store. Or the family lost its way by taking a wrong road on a trip. Refer to it briefly, asking how the child felt at the time. Then say:* In our story today we are going to meet Janey Brown, who is just three years old. Maybe you'll know how Janey feels.

LISTENING TOGETHER. Janey Brown felt like a very big girl. She went out of her yard to get her kitten, Taffy. But Taffy kept running all the way down the block. She crossed a street and was still going as fast as she could. Janey didn't want her kitten to get lost, so the faster the kitten ran the faster Janey ran.

Now Janey's legs were getting tired. Her knee was hurting where she had bumped it on the sidewalk. So Janey stopped and looked around. Nothing looked very friendly. She couldn't see her own house anymore, and she didn't see anyone she knew.

She decided she would go home. Poor Janey, she couldn't remember which way to go. She hurried down one street, but it wasn't the right one. She looked and looked until she was too tired to walk.

Janey was very frightened because she couldn't find the way home. She was thinking how much she wanted to be home with her mother. She sat crying on the curb. She was very sad because she had no friend to show her the way.

A car drove up, and a policeman got out. "What's the trouble, little girl?" he asked.

"I got lost," cried Janey.

"Maybe I can help you. Can you tell me your name?"

"I'm Janey Brown," she sobbed.

"Is Stephen Brown your father?" asked the policeman.

"Yes."

"Well, don't worry. Your father is my friend, and I know where you live. Get in my car and I'll have you home in a minute."

Soon Janey and the policeman were at the Brown home. You can imagine how happy the family was to have Janey found. After supper they sat together and talked about it.

"It was a good thing Janey's policeman friend found her and showed her the way home," said Bobby, Janey's big brother.

"Yes," said Mr. Brown. "It's nice to have friends. All the things that happened this afternoon remind me to talk about our other good Friend."

"I know whom you mean, Dad," interrupted Bobby. "You're talking about Jesus, aren't you?"

"That's right, Bobby," answered Father. "At one time all of us were something like Janey. We were lost because we didn't know the way to God. We had no way to our home in heaven. But then Jesus came into the world. Jesus became the Way to God. In God's Word Jesus says, 'I am the Way.' Trusting in Jesus is the only way we can come to God. When you trust in Jesus, you aren't lost from God anymore."

Janey sighed, "I'm glad I'm not lost anymore."

Father smiled and added, "We're glad, too, that you aren't lost, and we are all happy we know Jesus, the only Way to heaven."

TALKING TOGETHER. How did Janey feel when she was lost? How did Janey find the way home? Why were we like Janey once? Who is the only way to God and heaven? Tell how we can be sure we are on the way to God and heaven.

Hurt or Love?

By love serve one another. Galatians 5:13

BEGINNING TOGETHER. *Talk with children about times they were hurt. In the discussion bring out that sometimes people are hurt accidentally and other times they are hurt by others intentionally. Then say:* Today Bobby Brown learns something about hurting others.

LISTENING TOGETHER. Mrs. Brown was busy in the kitchen when Betty banged open the back door and called, "Mom, come quick! Bobby and that new boy from down the street are fighting."

By the time Mrs. Brown got to the back door she saw the new boy running home holding his head. Bobby was brushing himself off. "I guess I showed him who's boss around here," said Bobby angrily.

"After the way you treated him, he won't want to play with you anymore, Bobby," scolded Mother.

"I don't care," grumbled Bobby. "He was asking for it."

"Maybe you better tell me a little more about what happened."

"It was all his fault," said Bobby. "We were building roads for our model cars, and Don kept running his car on my place. So I just picked up his car and tossed it away. When it broke, Don got up and pushed me over; so I hit him. That's all."

"I think that's enough," answered Mother. "Bobby, you're forgetting something that's very important. We've talked about it before."

"I suppose you mean I shouldn't have started the trouble. But he really started it. I wasn't going to let him get so bossy," argued Bobby.

"I'm talking about something Dad read the other evening. Remember what the apostle Paul wrote: 'By love serve one another.'"

"Yes, I guess I remember. But what about Don? He wasn't showing any love to me," protested Bobby.

"We can't do anything about what Don did. But we can do something about your mistake. You could have been the one to show love first. When you hurt Don, you also sinned against God," said Mother sadly.

"I guess I was wrong, Mother," admitted Bobby. "I'm sorry I hurt Don. I don't like being in trouble."

Mother cautioned Bobby, "Sin always brings trouble. It makes us feel bad, just like you do now."

"But what should I do, Mother?"

"The first thing to do is ask God to forgive you," answered Mother. "He forgives you because Jesus suffered and died for you. He loves you very much."

"I love Him, too, Mother," smiled Bobby. "You know, I think I'll get Don a new car. I'll tell him this afternoon that I'm sorry."

"Good," said Mother. "Now you are doing what God told us to do: 'By love serve one another.'"

TALKING TOGETHER. What caused the trouble in the Browns' yard? Why was Bobby wrong to start trouble? Is it easy to show love to others? Why not? How did Bobby show love to Don?

PRAYING TOGETHER. *Dear Lord, I want to show love to others, but it is very hard to do it. Give me more of Jesus' love so I show more love to others. Help me to be kind when I play. Amen.*

Talking to a Friend

Pray without ceasing.   1 Thessalonians 5:17

BEGINNING TOGETHER. Who are some of your favorite friends in your neighborhood? Do you like to be with them? What are some of the things you do together? As we visit the Brown family today, we find that one of the family is missing. The one who is not there is Betty, the 7-year-old.

LISTENING TOGETHER. "Bobby, have you seen Betty?" asked Mother Brown. It was almost time for breakfast when Mrs. Brown discovered that Betty was not in the house.

"I think I saw her go over to the Schultzes a few minutes ago," answered Bobby.

"I hope she isn't bothering them so early in the morning. We can't wait for her. It's time to eat so you can be off to school."

The Browns prayed their table prayer and started eating. They had been eating a few minutes when Betty came in the back door singing. "Well," said Mr. Brown, "where have you been?"

Betty sat down at her place.

"I had to tell Mary something."

"Girls!" teased Bobby. "They're talking all the time."

"That's all right, Betty," said Mother; "I'm glad you have a nice friend like Mary."

"Let's get finished now," said Father as he reached for the Bible. "We want to have time for our morning prayer before we all have to leave."

"Oh, Daddy, I don't see why we have to take time this morning," complained Betty. "I promised Mary I would be right out."

"It will take only a few minutes, Betty," answered Father.

"Yes, but we prayed last night during our devotion,

and I did again when I went to bed, and we'll do it tonight again. I — "

"Betty, did you see Mary after supper last night?"

"Yes, but what has that got to do with praying?" answered Betty.

"And what was the first thing you wanted to do this morning?"

"I wanted to go over and see Mary, I guess, but I still don't see — "

"Why do you want to see her so often?" asked Father again.

"Daddy, you know she's my friend." Betty looked more puzzled all the time.

"I know what Daddy means," interrupted Bobby. "You want to hurry outside to be with your friend. But you are really forgetting your very best Friend — God."

"That's right, Bobby," said Father. "It is good to have friends, but they should never make us forget God. Talking with Him is most important because He sent Jesus to be our Savior. Praying once or twice isn't really enough. God tells us how often we should pray when He tells us in the Bible: 'Pray without ceasing.' "

"How could we do that, Daddy? We wouldn't have time to eat or sleep or anything," said little Jimmy.

"It means that we start and end the day with Him. All the time in between we feel God very close to us. We feel so close that we think about Him and talk to Him often. Let's start this day right by talking it over with God. Are you ready, Betty?" asked Father.

"Yes, Daddy, and I'm sorry I was in such a hurry. I'll always have time for God."

TALKING TOGETHER. Why did the Browns have to begin eating without Betty? Why was Betty in a hurry? What had she forgotten? What is the best way to start the day?

How many times should we pray? What does it mean to "pray without ceasing"?

PRAYING TOGETHER. *Dear God, You are always close to me. I love You more than my friends on earth because You are my God. You have made me and sent Jesus to be my Savior. Thank You for hearing me when I pray. Amen.*

I'm Sorry

Lord, be merciful to me, a sinner. Luke 18:13

BEGINNING TOGETHER. *Help the children recall times when they have done something wrong. Particularly bring out times when they tried to hide what they had done wrong. Then say:* In our story Jimmy tries to hide something. See if you have ever felt the way he does.

LISTENING TOGETHER. "Come, everyone, let's play that new game Jimmy got for his birthday," called Father Brown after supper. Bobby and Betty came running down the stairs from their rooms. Janey and Mother Brown came in from the kitchen.

"Where's Jimmy?" asked Mother.

"He's sitting on the front steps," Bobby answered. "He said he didn't want to play."

"That surely doesn't sound like our Jimmy," said Father. "He's been after me all week to play this with him. Is he sick?"

"He was fine when he came home from kindergarten this morning. He played in his room most of the afternoon," answered Mother.

"I think I'll see if he's all right." Father went to the front door. "You can start playing." Father went out the door and sat down beside Jimmy.

"How are you, Jimmy?"

"All right, I guess," mumbled Jimmy.

"Do you hurt anyplace?" asked Father.

"No, I feel all right," answered Jimmy.

"Did someone bother you then, son?"

"No."

"Something's wrong, Jimmy. You'll feel better if you tell me about it."

"But I can't tell you, Daddy. You'll get angry at me."

"Well, son, you aren't very happy right now. I think you had better talk to me. Now what happened?"

"All right, but I know you're going to be angry," mumbled Jimmy. "Mother told me never to sit on my bed and cut things for my scrapbook. But this afternoon I did it anyway, and I cut a hole in my bedspread."

"Jimmy, do you understand why your mother told you never to sit on your bed while using a scissors?"

"Yes, Daddy, and I'm really sorry. I've felt bad all afternoon."

"I know you're sorry, Jimmy, and I don't think you'll do it again. I forgive you, son, and I know Mother will forgive you, too. But you know there's Someone else who is waiting to forgive you. Do you know who that is?"

"I guess you mean God," answered Jimmy.

"That's right. When you didn't listen to your mother, you also sinned against God."

"Do you think He'll forgive me like you did, Daddy?"

"I'm sure He will. Once Jesus told a story about a very sinful man. He knew he had done many sins. One day he went to church and said, 'Lord, be merciful to me, a sinner.' He wanted God to forgive Him. We learn in this story that God did forgive the man. God loved him. And God loves you, too, Jimmy. He forgives you. We know this because Jesus lived and died to take away your sins."

"Daddy, I'm happy God forgives me. I feel better already."

TALKING TOGETHER. Why was Jimmy sad? How did he get to feel better? Do we feel good if we try to hide the bad things we do? What should we do if we do something wrong?

PRAYING TOGETHER. *Heavenly Father, I am sorry for the sins I do each day. Forgive me for Jesus' sake. Help me to stay away from doing wrong. Amen.*

Watch Out!

Watch and pray. Matthew 26:41

BEGINNING TOGETHER. *Encourage the family to recall rules they are to obey in the home. Let the children tell about times when the rules were broken. Then say:* What makes us break rules? Listen to our story today, and maybe Bobby Brown can help you find the answer.

LISTENING TOGETHER. Mr. Brown had just come home from work. As he went out the back door, he called to Bobby, "Do you want to help me wash the car before supper?"

"All right, Dad, I'll be there in a minute," answered Bobby from his room.

The two worked quietly for a while, and then Bobby asked, "What's wrong with me, Dad?"

"Nothing, as far as I know," answered Mr. Brown. "Did you have something on your mind, son?"

"Something happened this afternoon, and I don't understand it. Tommy came over after school and wanted me to go with him to watch the high school boys practice football. But Mom told me she didn't want me to go."

"Did you go, Bobby?"

"No, but I had it all figured out how I could sneak out of the yard and Mom would never know. I knew Mom wouldn't like it if I didn't listen to her. Yet I still wanted to go. What made me want to sneak off like that? Is there something wrong with me?"

"I don't think there's anything wrong with you, Bobby. I think you were in a big fight."

"A fight? Who, me?"

"Yes, you. Everyone has the same trouble, even children the size of little Janey. The trouble is with the devil. He tries to get you to sin. And you want to do what God says. The devil is very happy when he can talk you into doing something wrong."

"I didn't know the devil was working on me," said Bobby.

"We never see the devil, so sometimes we forget he's around to get us into trouble. Jesus knew it when He told His disciples to 'watch and pray.' That is the only way we can win the fight against the devil. We aren't strong enough by ourselves. We have to pray and ask God to help us. Only God can help us stay away from sinning and win against the devil."

"Are you sure God is stronger than the devil?"

"Yes, Bobby. Remember, the devil could not make Jesus sin in the desert. Jesus also won over the devil when He rose from the dead. He showed He was stronger than the devil."

"I'm always going to ask God to help me. I'm glad I won today," said Bobby.

"Remember, you didn't win alone. God and you won," smiled Father.

"I won't forget, Dad."

TALKING TOGETHER. Why did Bobby think something was wrong with him. Who was trying to make Bobby do something wrong? Are we strong enough to win over the devil? What does Jesus tell us we should do to win over the devil?

A Tray of Love

Honor thy father and thy mother. Ephesians 6:2, 3

BEGINNING TOGETHER. *Talk with the children about how God gives children parents to take care of them. Discuss ways they can show their love to their parents. Then say:* Let's see how the Brown children showed love to their parents.

LISTENING TOGETHER. "How are you feeling now, Mother?" asked Mr. Brown. Mrs. Brown had stayed in bed because of a bad cold.

"Oh, I should be all right by tomorrow."

"We want you to stay right there until you're feeling better. We're getting along fine," boasted Father.

"What are all those busy sounds coming from the kitchen? I'm getting very curious about them," said Mother.

"That's going to be a surprise for you," replied Father. "I was supposed to come up here and find out if you were ready for breakfast."

"Do you mean you fixed my breakfast for me?" laughed Mother.

"Oh, no. You know what kind of cook I am. The children have been busy working on something. I can't tell you what they're fixing; that's a secret. But I can tell you this much, you're going to have a tray full of love."

"What? Now I really am curious to find out what's going on around here."

Just then the bedroom door flew open, and Janey and

Jimmy bounced into the room. They couldn't stand still while they waited for Bobby and Betty to come with the tray.

"See, Mommy, we made it all by ourselves." Janey jumped up and down on one foot. "I put the plate and glass on the tray."

"And I put the cereal in the bowl," shouted Jimmy.

"Betty made the toast and I poured the juice," added Bobby proudly. "Everybody did something."

"See, didn't I tell you? It's a tray of love. Everyone did something for Mother because we love her," said Father.

"This all looks so good. Thank you, children. I am happiest because you remembered something you learned in Sunday school last Sunday. Remember what the Bible words were that we studied?"

"I remember," replied Betty. "Honor thy father and thy mother."

"What does honor mean?" asked Jimmy.

"I remember that," answered Bobby. "Our teacher said it means to do more than just obey. It means to show love, too. We want to show love because our hearts are filled with love for Jesus, our Savior."

"And we do love you, Mommy," said Janey, bouncing on the bed.

TALKING TOGETHER. What problem was in the Brown house one morning? What was the tray of love? Why was it called that? What does it mean to honor our parents? Can you tell how you can show love to your parents?

PRAYING TOGETHER. *Heavenly Father, I thank You for my mother and father. Help me show love for them by obeying them. Give me more love so that I will be happy to help them at home. Amen.*

Ready to Forgive

Thou, Lord, art good, and ready to forgive. Psalm 86:5

BEGINNING TOGETHER. *Show the children an article or picture in the newspaper of someone who has done something wrong. Then say:* Bobby Brown has some questions today about a picture he found in a newspaper.

LISTENING TOGETHER. Father Brown was reading his newspaper after dinner. Bobby finished helping Mother in the kitchen and came to the living room. "What did that man do, Dad?" asked Bobby as he looked over his father's shoulder at a man's picture in the paper.

"He took half a million dollars from his company," answered Father.

"Wow, that's a lot of money," said Bobby. "How much is half a million dollars?"

"Well, Bobby, if we piled it all up in one pile, it would be higher than you are."

"What are they going to do to him?" asked Bobby.

"Oh, I suppose they'll send him to prison to punish him."

"Dad, do you think God will forgive him for taking all that money?"

"Bobby, God answered your question in a beautiful psalm in the Bible. He had David write down these words: 'Thou, Lord, art good, and ready to forgive.' If this man in the newspaper is truly sorry and trusts in Jesus as his Savior, God will forgive him."

"I'm surely glad I'm not like that man. I've never done anything that bad," boasted Bobby proudly.

"Wait a minute, son," said Mr. Brown. "You sin every day, and every sin is bad. You need God's love just as much as this man."

"Well, I don't remember that I am so bad, Dad," said Bobby, frowning a little.

"How about this morning when Mother wanted you to make your bed before you went to school? Remember how you grumbled and didn't get it done? And think a minute, I heard you and Betty quarreling right before supper. I'm sure you know I'm right."

"I guess you're right, Dad. I'm glad God is ready to forgive me. I surely need it," answered Bobby.

"You're right, son; we all need God's forgiveness," said Father. "And Jesus made it all possible. He gave His life so your sins could be taken away."

"Dad, I'm glad we read the paper together. I learned a lot from that picture," said Bobby.

TALKING TOGETHER. What picture did Bobby see in the newspaper one evening? What Bible words did Mr. Brown use to show Bobby about God's forgiveness? Bobby didn't think he needed forgiveness as much as the sinful man. Tell if he was right. Do we need forgiveness? What Bible words tell us that God will forgive us?

PRAYING TOGETHER. *Heavenly Father, I know that I do wrong things every day. Sometimes I am not kind to my brothers and sisters. I don't listen to my mother and father the way I should. I am sorry. Forgive me for Jesus' love. Amen.*

Who Is Jesus?

This is the true God. 1 John 5:20

BEGINNING TOGETHER. If someone asked you, "Who is Jesus?" could you give a good answer? What could you tell someone about Jesus? Mr. Brown asks his family that today. Let's see if they answer it the way you did.

LISTENING TOGETHER. The Browns were on their way home from church one Sunday. They had had a special visitor at church that morning. A missionary had talked to the Sunday school children. Later he had preached the sermon in church.

As they were getting into the car, everyone seemed to be talking at once. "Dad, do you know what the missionary told us this morning?" asked Bobby.

"No, but it must have been interesting. Everyone has been talking since we got out of church," answered Mr. Brown.

"The missionary told us that when he goes to a new village or when he sees people in the mission hospital for the first time they ask him, 'Who is Jesus?' Imagine! They don't even know who He is," said Bobby shaking his head.

"I can hardly believe that they never heard His name," added Betty. "I've known about Jesus as long as I can remember."

"Yes, Betty, that's true. You've known about Jesus all your life. But many people don't know Him. Pretend you're the missionary. If someone would ask you, 'Who is Jesus?' how would you answer?"

"I would tell them that He makes me well when I am sick. Remember when the doctor had to come last winter? Jesus made me better then," replied Jimmy.

"I could tell them I don't get afraid when I think about Jesus. Last night, when we had the storm, I knew Jesus was right by my bed," smiled Janey.

"How about you, Betty? You said you've known Jesus for a long time. What would you say?" asked Mr. Brown.

"Well, let me see — oh, He listens to me when I pray, and He answers my prayers, too," answered Betty.

"I know something you forgot," interrupted Bobby. Jesus is my best Friend, who died for me. And He did it so all the bad things I do could be forgiven by God."

"Don't forget that He died but also rose again," added Mrs. Brown. "That's what makes Him so special."

"All of your answers were right, but you forgot the answer that makes all of these other things possible. In the Bible God talks about Jesus and says: 'This is the true God.' Jesus is God. He is able to heal us and protect us. He can answer our prayers. He became man so He could suffer for all the sins of everyone," said Mr. Brown.

"I love Jesus so much," said Betty. "I'm glad I know Him."

TALKING TOGETHER. What did the missionary tell about that surprised the Brown children? How did the Brown children answer the question, "Who is Jesus?" How would you answer the question, "Who is Jesus?"

PRAYING TOGETHER. *Dear Jesus, I know that You are God. Thank You for loving me so much You became a man to suffer and die for me. I love You more every day. Keep me close to You always. Amen.*

Sad Sounds

Forgive one another. Ephesians 4:32

BEGINNING TOGETHER. *Show a small piece of broken crayon to the family. Then say:* This looks very small, but it plays a big part in our story of the Brown family today.

LISTENING TOGETHER. Everything seemed happy in the Brown house even though the rain had been dripping all day outside. Betty had just come home from school and went singing up the stairs to her room.

Mrs. Brown was just thinking how nice it was to have such a cozy, happy home when she heard a loud bang upstairs. She could hear Betty running down the hall and crying, "Jimmy, Jimmy, why did you do it?" Then the door banged again, and Betty was in Jimmy's room shouting, "Why did you break my crayons?"

Jimmy shouted back, "I didn't break your old crayons."

"Yes, you did," answered Betty. "See them here."

"Well, I just used them a minute. You shouldn't be so selfish."

"You had no right to take my crayons," cried Betty. "I don't think you're very nice."

"I don't think you're nice either if you're going to be so selfish."

"Jimmy, you're terrible. I'm going to tell Mother," said Betty as she went down the stairs.

"Jimmy broke my — "

"Now just stop right there," interrupted Mother as Betty came banging down the stairs. "Before you get started telling me what Jimmy did, you better think about what you did."

"What I did? I didn't break anything, but that old Jimmy sure made a mess in my things," complained Betty.

"Come into the kitchen with me and get a glass of milk. Maybe if we talk for a minute, you'll see what you did," invited Mother.

"All right," mumbled Betty, "but I'm still angry at Jimmy."

"You know this afternoon the house seemed so happy until I heard all of those sad angry sounds from upstairs."

"But I couldn't let Jimmy just break my crayons and not say anything," said Betty.

"Why not? You could have told him how sad it made you. But you didn't have to start an angry argument. You know Jesus has told us that we should forgive one another."

"But that's hard to do, Mother."

"Yes, of course, it is; but you don't have to do it all by yourself. Jesus will help you to be forgiving. Just ask Him to help."

"I guess I see what you mean, Mother. Jimmy broke something and that was wrong. But I started an argument and that was wrong, too. I'm sorry I got so angry."

"Betty, God wants to forgive us when we do something wrong. He wants to forgive Jimmy and you, too, for the trouble this afternoon. That is why Jesus lived and died so you could have this forgiveness."

"Mother, God forgives me so often when I sin. I guess I should forgive, too. I'm going to share a few of my crayons with Jimmy. If he has a few, maybe he won't get into mine again."

TALKING TOGETHER. What were the sad sounds mother heard upstairs? Who was wrong — Jimmy or Betty? What did Jesus tell us to do when someone did something bad to us? Is it easy? How can we do it then?

PRAYING TOGETHER. *Dear God, fill my heart with Your love. Let me be ready to forgive my brothers and sisters when we have trouble. Amen.*

Strainer or Dipper?

Blessed are they that hear the Word of God and keep it.
Luke 11:28

BEGINNING TOGETHER. *Let the family examine a small tea strainer. Talk about the fact that water will run right through it. Then say:* As we watch the Brown family, see if you can find out why you sometimes are like the strainer.

LISTENING TOGETHER. It was such a warm afternoon that the Brown children had come in to ask a special favor of Mrs. Brown. "May we help make some punch for everyone?" asked Bobby.

"That sounds like a good idea," said Mrs. Brown. "I've been working this afternoon, and it's time for a little rest anyway."

All four of the Brown children helped. It was soon mixed in a large kettle. "Do you have enough glasses, Bobby, for all of your friends?" asked Mother.

"Yes, here are eight glasses. I'll put them on the table." Mother turned to Janey. "Could you please get a dipper from the drawer? I want to put the punch in the glasses."

"Here, Mommy, is this what you want?" Janey was trying to be a good helper.

"Oh, no," laughed Betty. "Look what Janey brought. She brought you a strainer."

"Mom, how are you going to get any punch in the glasses with that strainer?" giggled Bobby.

"That's enough, children," scolded Mother. "Come here, Janey. This is a strainer and not a dipper. See? When we put the strainer into the punch, it all runs right through. None of it stays in so we can pour it into the glasses. We need the dipper. It's like a cup with a long handle on it. When we put it into the punch, the punch stays in it. Then we can fill the glasses," explained Mother. "Now let's get busy. And no more laughing at Janey, children."

As the Brown family was eating supper, Mr. Brown said, "Jimmy was telling me that Janey learned what a dipper is." Jimmy began to laugh, but Mr. Brown looked up quickly and said, "That's enough, Jimmy. It isn't that funny, and besides, I'm afraid you're like Janey's strainer." Jimmy looked down at his plate and didn't say anything.

"God says in His Word, 'Blessed are they that hear the Word of God and keep it.' It isn't enough just to hear it. We must do what it says. Some people *hear* what God wants them to do, but they don't *do* anything about it. They're like strainers. Nothing stays with them."

"Was I a strainer, Mommy?" asked Jimmy.

"I'm afraid you were. You know God wants you to obey your parents. But today when I told you not to laugh at Janey, you didn't obey," said Mrs. Brown.

Mr. Brown looked at Jimmy. "I hope you can be like some people who hear God's Word and remember it. They learn of God's love when He sent Jesus to be our Savior. They hear what God wants them to do. Then they do it because of Jesus' love. They're like a dipper. They keep some of God's Word and are able to use it."

"I'm sorry, Janey. We both had something to learn today," said Jimmy.

TALKING TOGETHER. Can a strainer hold much water? When are people who hear God's Word like a strainer? When are they like a dipper? Is it enough to just hear God's Word? What must we also do with it? Why will we want to do what God says?

PRAYING TOGETHER. *Lord, God, from Your Word I have learned that You love me. Let this love fill my heart that I will want to do the things You say. Help me, O Lord. Amen.*

Never Alone

I am with you always. Matthew 28:20

BEGINNING TOGETHER. Did you ever wake up in the middle of the night when everyone else was sleeping? How did you feel? The night is so quiet, and you feel that no one else is near. Maybe you know what it is like to be alone at other times. In our story today Jimmy finds out what it is like to be alone.

LISTENING TOGETHER. The Brown house was very dark because it was the middle of the night. All of the Browns were sleeping. Well, almost all of the Browns were sleeping — Jimmy was sitting straight up in bed.

He listened and he couldn't hear his mother and father. He looked toward the door, and there was no light shining in the hall. Jimmy felt so alone. He sat there wanting someone else to be with him. Jimmy thought maybe he could try to go back to sleep, so he snuggled down in the covers and pulled the blankets over his head. He was just beginning to feel warm and cozy when he heard something strange outside his window. He sat up in bed again and felt so alone.

When the noise came again, Jimmy began to cry, "Mommy, Daddy."

Mrs. Brown heard him cry and hurried down the hall from her bedroom. "What's the matter, son?" she asked.

"I don't like to be alone, Mommy. Something is outside my window," cried Jimmy.

"Let's see what's making that noise," answered Mother as she went toward the window.

Jimmy was feeling very brave, now that his mother was there, so he followed her.

"Look, Jimmy, the big noise is just the branch of that tree rubbing against the window. You don't have to be afraid," said Mother as she picked him up in her arms.

"Mommy, don't leave me here alone," said Jimmy as he hugged his mother very tight.

"Don't be afraid, son. Daddy and I are right down the hall," said Mrs. Brown.

"But no one is right here with me," said Jimmy.

"Are you really alone, Jimmy? Do you remember the time Jesus was saying goodbye to His disciples. He finished telling them what they were supposed to do. He knew they might at times be afraid, so He told them, 'Lo, I am with you always.' "

"Did Jesus mean me, too, Mommy?" asked Jimmy.

"Yes, Jesus meant you and everyone who trusts in Him,"

answered Mother. "You don't have to be afraid here in your bedroom. Jesus is right with you every minute."

"I love Jesus, Mommy," smiled Jimmy.

"Jesus loves you, too, Jimmy. That's why He is with you. That's the reason, too, that He was willing to suffer and die for you. Let's talk to Jesus for a few minutes. Then I know you can go back to sleep." Mother tucked the covers around him.

"All right, Mommy. I feel good now."

TALKING TOGETHER. What made Jimmy afraid one night? Was Jimmy really alone? What should we think about when we are afraid or alone? Why did Jesus suffer and die for us?

PRAYING TOGETHER. *Lord Jesus, I feel safe and happy when I know You are with me. When I feel afraid or lonely, help me to remember that You are with me always. Amen.*

(Today mother or father adds a sentence prayer about a particular fear of some member of the family. Ask God to help overcome this fear. Children could repeat prayer.)

Showing Love

Love your enemies; do good to them which hate you. Luke 6:27

BEGINNING TOGETHER. *Talk about children in the neighborhood who are the cause of trouble or who are unusually cruel in their play. Perhaps there is a neighborhood bully who causes trouble for others. Then say:* God knows there is this kind of person in the world. God calls them our enemies. Today Bobby learns how to treat them.

LISTENING TOGETHER. Bobby had just come into the kitchen after school. "I'm home, Mom," he called as he opened the cookie jar. Bobby couldn't find any cookies, but on the table he saw two pieces of pie on a plate. "Mmm, that looks good. Mom, may I have a piece of pie, please?"

"I'm sorry, Bobby. This is for Mr. Rogers next door," said Mother.

"What?" grumbled Bobby, looking very disgusted. "Why do you want to take something over to that old crab?"

"Bobby, that's no way to talk about our neighbor," scolded Mother. "Mr. Rogers has been sick. I want to go over to see how he is. I think he would enjoy having something special once."

"I still don't see why you have to take that to him. I would like it just as much as he would. If I know Mr. Rogers, he'll probably complain that there isn't enough sugar in it or something. He's always complaining about what we do."

"Just because Mr. Rogers isn't kind doesn't mean that we should be unkind, too," said Mother.

"But, Mom, don't you remember how he always fusses at Dad for things Dad never does? He always yells at us when our ball rolls on his lawn," complained Bobby.

"Bobby, can you remember what God tells us to do to people like Mr. Rogers who are not kind to us?" asked Mother.

"Let's see, I think we are to love them. But the way he acts, it would be much easier just to let him alone," said Bobby.

"It might be easier. But because of Jesus' love we want to do what God says. God told us: 'Love your enemies; do good to them which hate you.' "

"It still sounds like a hard thing to show love to Mr. Rogers," said Bobby, shaking his head.

"It wasn't an easy thing for Jesus to suffer and die for us, Bobby. But He did it because He loved us. We'll show love to Mr. Rogers because our hearts are filled with Jesus' love. I know what you can do, Bobby. Come with me when I go over to his house. I think you'll be surprised."

An hour passed. Bobby and his mother are coming home from the neighbor's. "Mom, I just wouldn't have believed it. Mr. Rogers actually smiled when you gave him that pie. He seemed almost nice."

"That's right, son. God's way of treating people is right. When we show love, we show them Jesus' love. That makes a difference."

TALKING TOGETHER. Where was Bobby's mother going to take the pie? Why was Bobby unhappy about it? How does God want us to treat people who are not kind? Why are we to obey God and show kindness to our enemies?

PRAYING TOGETHER. *Dear God, fill my heart with Jesus' love. I want to follow Your Word and be kind to my enemies. But I need Your help to show this love. Amen.*

(Today father or mother adds sentence prayer for someone who is sick. It might be a relative, friend, or neighbor. Perhaps pray for the sick in general. Children repeat prayer.)

Washed Clean

Arise and be baptized and wash away thy sins. Acts 22:16

BEGINNING TOGETHER. *Ask the children if they remember seeing a baby baptized in church. Talk about it. Then say:* Today Jimmy finds out something about Baptism.

LISTENING TOGETHER. "Jimmy, if you'll help me put my wash into the dryer, we'll go over to Mrs. Sawyer's house to see their new baby," said Mother as she went to the basement.

"Here I come," said Jimmy.

"My, I wonder what happened to this wash," said Mrs. Brown as she looked into her washing machine. "These clothes are still dirty even though they have finished washing."

"Did you put some soap in the machine, Mommy?" asked Jimmy.

"Of course I did, Jimmy. Don't you remember we put the clothes in and then the telephone rang and — you're right. I did forget the soap when the telephone rang. We'll just leave them right here until we get back from our visit."

In a few minutes Mrs. Brown had walked with Jimmy and Janey to visit Mrs. Sawyer.

"He sure is tiny," whispered Jimmy as Mrs. Sawyer held the baby.

"All babies are very tiny when they are only two weeks old," laughed Mrs. Brown.

"But he isn't too tiny to go to church," said Mrs. Sawyer. "Danny is going to be baptized this Sunday."

"What does it mean to be baptized, Mommy?" asked Janey.

"Janey, you remember that sometimes people bring a little baby to the front of the church. There is a little basin of water. Then the pastor puts some of the water on the head of the baby and says some words that Jesus used."

"But why do they do it, Mommy?" asked Janey.

"I think part of the answer is one I remember from God's Word: 'Be baptized and wash away your sins.' When a baby is baptized, his sins are washed away."

"When I wash my hands, do I wash away my sins, too, Mommy?" asked Jimmy.

"No, it doesn't work that way, Jimmy. The water alone can't wash sins away. It is God's Word that is in and with the water that does it."

"You mean it's kind of like your wash this morning," said Jimmy thinking very hard.

"Like my wash? What do you mean?" Mother looked puzzled.

"You know your clothes didn't get clean when you washed them in plain water. You needed the soap with the water before the dirt was washed away."

"I guess you could say it's a little like that," smiled Mother. "It makes us happy to remember our Baptism. We know that our sins were washed away. But it is much more than that, too. When we are baptized, we become God's children. We belong to God. He forgives our sins because Jesus lived and died for us."

"Was I baptized, Mommy?" asked Jimmy.

"Yes, son; and you belong to God now. When you sin, you can remember that you belong to God. You remember that you were baptized. God wants to forgive you because of Jesus."

Little Danny made a noise as his mother moved him. Janey stood very close to him and whispered quietly, "Look, Danny is happy to know he's going to be baptized Sunday."

TALKING TOGETHER. Why was Danny's mother taking him to church? What was going to happen to Danny when he was baptized? Jimmy's mother told him that the water alone doesn't wash away sins. What does wash them away? To whom do you belong after you are baptized?

PRAYING TOGETHER. *Dear God, I became Your child when I was baptized. When I become sad, help me remember I belong to You. Amen.*

(Today father or mother says a sentence prayer thanking God for forgiving our sins. Children repeat prayer.)

The Biggest Why

Christ Jesus came into the world to save sinners. 1 Timothy 1:15

BEGINNING TOGETHER. *Ask the children what they do when they want to know something. Bring out in discussion that they often ask the question "why?" Then say:* Little Janey in our story is trying to find out about things, too.

LISTENING TOGETHER. "Daddy, why is our garage painted white?" asked Janey.

"Because your mother and I decided we liked that color," Mr. Brown answered as he finished sweeping the sidewalk.

"Why are you sweeping the sidewalk?" asked Janey again.

"Because it doesn't look very nice with all the dirt on it. Janey, could you put your tricycle in the garage?" asked Father.

"Why, Daddy?"

"It's going to rain and we don't want it to get wet. That's fine, Janey. Come now, let's go in. And don't ask me why. Your mother just called us in to eat supper," smiled Father.

The Brown family sat down to eat. After the prayer there wasn't much talking because everyone was so hungry. Janey stopped eating and asked, "Why do I have to drink milk?"

"Milk is a good food that helps your body grow strong. You like milk, so don't worry about it," urged Mother.

Mrs. Brown served dessert.

"Why don't I get as much ice cream as Bobby, Mommy?"

"You get just as much as you should for a girl your size. When you are Bobby's size, you will get more."

Father looked around the table. "Is everyone finished eating? Bobby, please get our Bible. We'll have a short time of talking with Jesus before we leave the table."

"Good," said Betty. "What will we talk about tonight?"

"Janey gave me an idea," replied Father. "She's been asking questions all day. Every time Mother or I turned around, there was Janey asking, 'Why?' Tonight I'm going to begin by asking you what is the biggest why."

"What do you mean by that, Dad?" asked Bobby.

"I want to know what is the most important question to us," answered Father. "It is: Why did Jesus come into the world? What would you say, Betty?"

"I guess He came into the world because He loved us," said Betty.

"Yes, that would be one answer. How about you, Bobby? Can you give us an answer?" asked Father again.

"I think it is because He wanted to die for us."

"Now we are very close to the answer. I want to read you the answer that God gives us in the Bible. He says: 'Christ Jesus came into the world to save sinners.' "

"What is a sinner, Daddy?" asked Janey.

"A sinner is any person who does not obey God all the time. You are a sinner, Bobby is a sinner, Betty and Jimmy are sinners, too."

"Are you a sinner, Daddy?" asked Janey.

"Yes, everyone in the whole world is a sinner," replied Father. "We all need Jesus to take our sins away. We all need Jesus to save us. It makes us happy to know that Jesus did that for all of us when He died and rose again."

TALKING TOGETHER. How was Janey bothering her family? What was the biggest question that Father asked? Can you answer the question why Jesus came into the world? Who are sinners?

PRAYING TOGETHER. *Heavenly Father, I know that I sin every day. I am sorry that I don't always do what you want me to do. Thank you for sending Jesus into the world to save me. Amen.*

(Today father or mother adds a sentence prayer for missionaries who are telling people around the world why Jesus came. Children repeat prayer.)

Who Is Stronger?

With God nothing shall be impossible. Luke 1:37

BEGINNING TOGETHER. *Ask the children who they think is stronger: mothers or fathers. Talk about things fathers can do better than mothers. Then say:* As we find the Brown family, we see that Bobby is having an argument about how strong his father is.

LISTENING TOGETHER. "My father can do more than your father," shouted Bobby.

"He cannot," answered Paul Smith. "My father can throw a football from here to my house."

"That's nothing. My dad can build things. He made a neat little desk for my room," boasted Bobby.

"So what? My dad is so strong he could push over that tree with one little shove."

"Well, my dad can lift up the front of our car with one hand."

While the boys were arguing, they didn't see that Mr. Brown had come into the backyard with Mr. Smith. "Wait a minute, boys. It sounds like you've gone far enough with those stories. Before you know it, you'll have Mr. Smith and me flying without wings or something," cautioned Mr. Brown.

Mr. Smith sat down on the grass. "Let's sit down here a minute and find out just what is the matter."

"Paul said his father could do more than you could, Dad, and that isn't true," complained Bobby.

"It is true, isn't it, Dad?" argued Paul.

"Now just stop a minute," interrupted Mr. Brown. "We don't want you two to get started all over again."

Mr. Brown turned to Mr. Smith and asked, "How are we going to settle this? I guess I could start by saying that you do play football better than I do."

33

"I'll have to tell Paul that you are better working with tools than I'll ever be," added Mr. Smith.

"The real answer is that Mr. Smith can do some things better and I can do other things better," said Mr. Brown.

"And don't forget, neither one of us can do everything."

"That's right," agreed Mr. Brown. "If you want to find someone who can do everything, you have to look to God. Remember, in His Word it says: 'With God nothing shall be impossible.' "

"That is a very important thing to remember," smiled Mr. Smith. "God can do anything. Nothing is too hard. He created the world. He takes care of it. He watches over each of us and gives us what we need. He listens to our prayers and helps us with our problems. We don't have to worry about anything, because we know God can do anything."

Paul thought for a moment and then added quietly: "God is so great and so powerful, I think I would almost be afraid to bother Him."

"No, we don't have to feel that way. Jesus suffered and died for us so that we can go to God anytime. He wants to help us," said Mr. Brown.

"I'm happy to have a good father with me and a strong Father like God in heaven," smiled Bobby.

TALKING TOGETHER. Who was stronger — Mr. Brown or Mr. Smith? Who is the only One who can do anything? Why shouldn't we be afraid to talk with God?

PRAYING TOGETHER. *Heavenly Father, You are so strong that I never have to worry about anything. You are stronger than any man. You are stronger than storms. You will take care of me, I know. Amen.*

(Today father or mother says a sentence prayer asking God to give everyone in the family a stronger faith in God. Children repeat prayer.)

Is Your Light Shining?

Let your light shine. Matthew 5:16

BEGINNING TOGETHER. *Let the family experiment with a flashlight. Let them discover if light will shine through glass or paper. Then have each try to shine the light through his hand. Then say:* As we find Janey Brown, we see that she is trying to find out about light, too.

LISTENING TOGETHER. Everyone was busy. Bobby, Betty, and Jimmy were playing out in the yard. Mr. Brown hadn't come home from work yet, and Mrs. Brown was in the kitchen. After a while Mrs. Brown began to wonder what Janey was doing. She had been so quiet.

Mrs. Brown went to the playroom and opened the door softly. There on the floor was Janey with Father's flashlight. As Mother watched, Janey took the flashlight, turned it on, and put it against her hand. The light made Janey's hand glow red.

Janey turned and saw Mother. "Look, Mommy, my hand shines."

Just then Bobby came in for some toys. "I see Janey is really doing what Pastor King told us to do yesterday in church," he teased.

"What do you mean, son?"

Bobby smiled, "He told us to let our light shine."

"Now, Bobby, you know Pastor King didn't mean that. Remember he read some words that Jesus said: 'Let your light shine.' But he said it was not like the light that we turn on in our house when it gets dark outside. It's a special kind of light."

"What kind of light, Mommy?" asked Janey.

"When God says, 'Let your light shine,' He means to let your love for Jesus show in everything you do. Our sins were washed away when Jesus died for us. We love Him, don't we?"

"I love Jesus," smiled Janey.

"I love Him, too, Mom," Bobby added.

"I know we all love Jesus. When we love Him we try to do the things He wants us to do. We listen to mother and father. We are kind to others. We tell others about how Jesus loves us. When other people see that, they know something special has happened to us. They say, 'That girl or that boy is different. He must love Jesus.' Then your light is shining."

Janey smiled, "See, Bobby, Mommy says I'm shining."

TALKING TOGETHER. What was Janey doing with the flashlight? What does it mean to "let your light shine"? What are some things you can do so people will know that you love Jesus and He loves you?

PRAYING TOGETHER. *Dear God, I love You so much. Help me show how much I love You in everything I do. Help me be kind and loving to others. Make me brave so I tell about Jesus' love. Amen.*

(Father or mother adds a sentence prayer asking God to help let our love for Jesus show in the way we behave toward others in the family. Children may repeat prayer.)

When Sadness Makes Us Glad

All things work together for good to them that love God.
Romans 8:28

BEGINNING TOGETHER. *Help the family recall when a member of the family was very ill. Talk about how the family feels when there is sickness. Then say:* There are many other things that happen that make us sad. Sometimes we wonder why they happen to us. Jimmy Brown was wondering about this, too, one day.

LISTENING TOGETHER. The Brown home was usually a happy place. But right now we find that there is some sadness there. Mr. Brown is in the hospital. The doctor says he will be able to come home in a few days, but the Browns have missed their father.

Jimmy had just come home from kindergarten and found his mother working in the yard. He sat down beside her in the warm sunshine and asked, "Mommy, why did God let Daddy get sick?"

Mrs. Brown looked at Jimmy a minute. "Jimmy, it is sometimes hard to find the right answer to all your questions. Maybe I can help you answer it for yourself by looking at this bush. Do you know what this is?"

"Sure, Mommy, that's a rose bush. It's the one with the pretty pink flowers on it in spring," answered Jimmy.

"That's right, son. Now watch what I have to do to this plant," said Mother as she took a sharp tool and began to cut off a branch.

"Mom, stop! You're hurting that plant," shouted Jimmy.

"It's all right, Jimmy. I have to cut the plant so that it is strong next year. If I would just let it grow, the plant would not be strong. Next spring the flowers would not be pretty. By cutting off some of the branches, it will grow stronger and give us beautiful flowers."

"You're really helping it, then, aren't you, Mommy?"

"Yes, I'm really helping it. Now can you see how this plant can help answer the question you asked?"

"You mean about why God let Daddy get sick?" asked Jimmy. "I still don't know."

"How often did you pray every day when Daddy was in the hospital?"

"Oh, I don't know. But I know we all prayed a lot of times."

"I think all of us felt very close to God during these last days. We knew He would do what was best for Daddy.

We trusted in Him so much. Now that Daddy is getting better, we all feel so good."

"Mommy, I love God."

"I know you do, Jimmy. Sometimes things that make us sad make our love for God stronger. God tells us in the Bible: 'All things work together for good to them that love God.' Even though it looks very sad for a little while, God promises that it will work out for our good."

"I'm glad God will take care of me," said Jimmy.

TALKING TOGETHER. Why were the Browns sad? Did Mother hurt the plant by cutting it? What should we remember when sad things happen in our lives?

PRAYING TOGETHER. *Heavenly Father, when I am sad, help me remember that You will help me. Fill my heart with love for You so that I always trust You. Amen.*

(Father or mother adds a sentence prayer asking God to keep us healthy if it is His will. Children may repeat prayer.)

Removing Stains

The blood of Jesus Christ, His Son, cleanseth us from all sin.
1 John 1:7

BEGINNING TOGETHER. *Talk about some of the problems children have when they try to help their parents paint. Talk about how hard it is to remove paint stains from hands and clothing. Then say:* Today Bobby is going to have trouble with some paint.

LISTENING TOGETHER. Bobby and his father were in the backyard painting the fence. They had been working for an hour or so, and Bobby was getting tired. He finally sat down and said, "I didn't know painting a fence was such hard work."

Father laughed and answered, "Looking at you I am not sure if you were painting the fence or painting yourself."

Bobby looked at his hands and clothes, "I guess I'm a little messy. Will this stuff come off, Dad?"

"It will take some hard rubbing, but I think you'll get most of it off. There now, it looks like we're finished. Come along, Bobby, we'll get to work on you now." Father closed the pail of paint.

Father and Bobby went into the house and began to clean up. As they scrubbed, Father asked, "Bobby, did you have a chance to ask Tom to come to Sunday school with you tomorrow?"

"Yes, Dad, I asked him yesterday at school. Tom said that he didn't need Sunday school." Bobby frowned a little.

"That's too bad," said Father. "Tom doesn't know that he needs Jesus. Tom is like many people today. They're so sure they can do everything by themselves."

"What can I do to help Tom?" asked Bobby.

"We'll have to think about it. Maybe there is some way you can help Tom see he really needs Jesus. He probably believes that if he tries to be very good, God will love him and forgive him."

"Dad, if Tom tried very hard to do good, could he make his sins go away?"

"No, son. The wrong things we do, our sins, are not like the paint on your hands. If you scrub very hard, the paint comes off. But our sins also stain us. No matter how hard we work, no matter how many good things we try to do, the sins are still there. The Bible tells us the only way they can be cleaned away: 'The blood of Jesus Christ, His Son, cleanseth us from all sin.' "

"I remember learning that. Jesus died for me to take my sins away, didn't He?"

"That's right, Bobby. Now that your sins are taken away, you can come to God and not be afraid. You know

He loves you. Because of Jesus' love He will help you stay away from sin. That's a wonderful thing to think about."

"It is, Dad. But I want Tom to know about it, too. I'm going to ask him again."

TALKING TOGETHER. What work were Mr. Brown and Bobby doing? What trouble did Bobby have with the paint? Are our sins like the paint on Bobby? Why not? Who is the only One who can take our sins away? How did He do it for us?

PRAYING TOGETHER. *Lord Jesus, thank You for taking my sins away. Help me to remember this every day and tell others about it. Amen.*

(Father or mother adds a sentence prayer for those who don't know Jesus as their Savior. Ask God to use the family to tell others of His love. Children may repeat prayer.)

Alive Again

Because I live, you shall live also. John 14:19

BEGINNING TOGETHER. Do you know someone who has died? We often feel sad when someone dies. But as we hear about the Brown family today, we find that we can be happy also about death.

LISTENING TOGETHER. Everything was quiet in the Brown house. No one was sleeping, but still you could not hear a sound. The Brown family was feeling a little sad because a few hours ago their kind neighbor across the street had died.

"I'm sure going to miss Grandma Malone. She always had time to talk to me," said Bobby sadly.

"Me, too," agreed Betty. "I liked it when she would tell stories about the time she was a little girl."

"I liked her cookies," added Janey.

"Yes, we are all going to miss Grandma Malone. Right now we feel sad because we won't have her with us anymore. But don't forget there is a happy side to death, too."

"I'm afraid to die like Grandma Malone did," said Jimmy with a troubled look in his eyes.

"Jimmy, maybe you can learn about the happy part of dying. Do you remember that Jesus was on the cross? Do you remember how He suffered and finally died?"

"Yes, Mommy."

"He died to take away your sins. Do you remember what happened after Jesus died?"

Betty interrupted. "I know. They took His body and put it in the grave. That was sad, too."

"But the next part of the story is the happiest story in the world. Jesus rose from the dead. He came alive again," added Bobby.

"Yes, that is a happy story. Jesus showed that He is God. He is stronger than death. Later He made a promise to all who love Him. He said: 'Because I live you shall live also.' "

"See, Jimmy, we don't have to be afraid to die," said Bobby. "Jesus is stronger than death."

Jimmy thought a moment. "Mommy, does that mean Grandma Malone is living right now?"

"Yes, she is living with Jesus. That is the happy part of dying that I talked about. Jesus is alive and we will live, too."

TALKING TOGETHER. Why were the Browns sad? What was the happy part of dying that Mother showed Jimmy? What words of Jesus could make us feel happier if we are afraid of death? What happens to people who love Jesus when they die?

PRAYING TOGETHER. *Lord Jesus, sometimes I am very sad when I think about someone dying. Never let me be afraid. I love You and I know I'll live with You when I die. Amen.*

(Father or mother adds a sentence prayer for older people who, like Grandma Malone, will soon be in heaven with Jesus. Ask God to make their love strong so they won't feel afraid. Children may repeat prayer.)

Is It True?

Thy Word is true. John 17:17

BEGINNING TOGETHER. What is a lie? When someone tells you a lie, it usually makes you angry, doesn't it? Whenever that person talks to you again, you don't know whether you should believe him or not. Janey felt like this after Bobby and Betty kept teasing her.

LISTENING TOGETHER. Betty and Bobby are like many brothers and sisters. They like to tease their little sister, Janey. They try to fool her whenever they can. Once they tried to make her eat a plastic apple. Another day they took her doll and hid it in a closet.

Today the children are playing together on their swings. "Where's Bobby?" asked Jimmy.

"He's in the house helping Mother," answered Betty as she went swinging as high as she could. "I wish I could fly as high as that bird way up there," she said.

"I know someone who can fly that high," shouted Bobby as he came running out to the swings. "It's Uncle Bill, and he's coming here tomorrow."

"Good," said Betty. "Uncle Bill always tells us such nice stories."

Janey slowly shook her head. "I don't think he's coming."

"Really, Janey, Mom said Uncle Bill would be here to-morrow afternoon. He called just a few minutes ago."

"No, you're just fooling again. Uncle Bill won't come. I'm going to ask Mommy." Janey ran to the house with Bobby coming along behind.

"Mommy, is Uncle Bill really coming tomorrow?"

"Yes, Janey, it's true. Uncle Bill will be coming to-morrow to spend a few days with us. Isn't that good news?"

"See, Janey, I told you he was coming. Why didn't you believe me?"

"Bobby, that's a good question," said Mother. "Why didn't Janey believe you?"

"Well, I don't know —" mumbled Bobby.

"I think you really know. You haven't always told Janey the truth. This time Janey didn't know if you were telling the truth or if you were fooling again. She couldn't trust you."

Janey gave her mother a big hug. "I know that God and Mommy always tell the truth."

"I'm glad you feel that way, Janey," smiled Mother, "but mothers can make mistakes, too. You're right about God. We can always trust what He says in His Word because we read, 'Thy Word is true.' "

"We can believe every word, can't we, Mom," said Bobby.

"That's right. We can believe it when God tells us that He loves us. We can believe it when He tells us that He has forgiven our sins for Jesus' sake. We can believe it when He tells us that He is watching over us just like a father."

TALKING TOGETHER. Why didn't Janey believe Bobby? Who were the ones Janey thought she could trust? What words from the Bible tell us that we can believe God? What are some of the important things we can believe that God has told us?

PRAYING TOGETHER. *Dear God, I trust You and know I can believe everything You say. I am happy because You have said You love me and forgive my sins. Amen.*

(Father or mother says a sentence prayer thanking God for the Bible so we may learn about our Savior Jesus. Children may repeat prayer.)

Powerful Jesus

All power is given unto Me in heaven and in earth.
Matthew 28:18

BEGINNING TOGETHER. Have you ever seen men building a road or a large new building? What kind of machines do they use? Some of the machines are so very big, and they lift great piles of dirt as if they were feathers. These machines are very strong. Jimmy in our story today is talking to his Uncle Bill about some powerful machines.

LISTENING TOGETHER. The Browns were very happy to have a visitor in their house. Their Uncle Bill, who was in the Air Force, was staying with them for a few days. The children were very proud of their uncle, who could fly big jet airplanes.

After supper Uncle Bill and Jimmy were sitting together. Uncle Bill was showing Jimmy a picture of the plane he flew. "That sure is a big airplane, Uncle Bill. Could it carry our whole family?"

Uncle Bill laughed. "Jimmy, this plane could carry all of you and all of your furniture and your car. And then it would still have room left."

"Wow, that is a strong airplane," said Jimmy with his eyes wide. "It must be the strongest thing in the whole world."

"No, I've seen some machines stronger than my airplane,

Jimmy. I've been at a place where they send up the big rockets. These rockets are stronger than my airplane. They lift thousands and thousands of pounds of rockets right up high into the sky. They lift them so high you can't see them. They're the strongest things man has ever built."

Bobby came into the room just then. "I'll bet I know something stronger, Uncle Bill."

"What is that, Bobby?"

"I know Jesus is stronger," smiled Bobby.

"You're right, Bobby. You had me guessing for a minute. It's a good thing for us to remember. Sometimes when I'm flying my big plane I think about how powerful Jesus is. It makes me happy to know He is so strong. I don't have to worry about anything. I like to remember a verse from the Bible when Jesus says, 'All power is given unto Me in heaven and in earth.' "

"I didn't know that big men who could fly airplanes loved Jesus, too," said Jimmy.

"Jimmy, everyone needs Jesus. We need Him to take our sins away. We all need Jesus, who is so strong He can take care of us."

"I'm glad we both love Him so much," smiled Jimmy. "He takes care of you way up in the sky, and He takes care of me right here at home."

TALKING TOGETHER. Who was the visitor at the Browns' house? What was Uncle Bill's job? What were some of the strong machines Uncle Bill told about? Who did Bobby say was stronger? Why does it make us happy to know that Jesus is so strong?

PRAYING TOGETHER. *Lord Jesus, You are so strong and I am small and weak. Stay close by me and watch over me every day. Amen.*

(Help one of the children say a sentence prayer asking God to also watch over relatives and friends who live at some distance from the family.)

Carrying the News

Go and tell the good news to all people. Mark 16:15

BEGINNING TOGETHER. *Let the family talk about the different ways to get a message to a grandparent or other relative who lives far away. It might travel by mail, by telephone, or by other means. Then say:* In cities there are people who carry a message from one place to another. They are called messengers. Did you know that you are a messenger? See if you can find what news you are to carry.

LISTENING TOGETHER. The Brown family was all busy working around the house. Bobby was picking up the magazines in the living room when he saw a man coming to the front door. "Someone is coming, Mom," called Bobby. "I'll see what he wants."

When Bobby opened the front door, the man asked, "Is this the home of Stephen Brown?"

"Yes, sir; he's my father," answered Bobby.

"I have a telegram here for him. Could you please call your mother?"

"Yes, right away." Bobby hurried to the kitchen. "Mom, a man wants to give you something."

"Thank you, Bobby." Mother went quickly to the front door. "Let's see, am I supposed to sign your book here?"

"That's right." The messenger handed Mother an envelope. "Here is your telegram."

"Read it, Mom; it must be important," said Betty.

"Let's see — oh, this is good news. It's from Uncle Bill. He just wanted to let us know that he arrived safely 'way up in Alaska in his airplane."

"How did the man get Uncle Bill's telegram?" asked Jimmy.

"Uncle Bill sent it by wire to an office here in our town. Then the man wrote it down and brought it to us."

"I'm glad he brought us such good news. I think I want to be a messenger with good news when I get big," said Jimmy.

"You're a messenger right now," smiled Mother.

"Who? Jimmy?" laughed Bobby.

"I'm not teasing. You're a messenger too, Bobby. In fact, all of us are messengers. We all are carrying good news."

Jimmy looked puzzled. "What good news do I have, Mommy?"

"The good news that God loves you and has forgiven your sins for Jesus' sake."

"Oh, I know all about that good news. But a messenger has to tell someone. Who am I supposed to tell?" asked Bobby.

"God said in His Word, 'Go and tell the good news to all people.' You should tell everyone you know. Remember how happy it made us to hear from Uncle Bill? You can make people happy when they hear about how much God loves them."

"I'm going to see if Steve is home. I never told him the good news yet," called Jimmy as he went out the back door.

TALKING TOGETHER. Who came to the Brown house one day? What did he have? Who else in the Brown family were messengers? What message were they to carry? Who in your family is to be a messenger? Can you think of some people you could tell about Jesus?

PRAYING TOGETHER. *Heavenly Father, use me as a messenger to bring the good news of Your love to other people. Make me happy to tell others of Jesus. Amen.*

(Help one of the children say a sentence prayer asking God to send missionaries to many lands to be messengers for Him.)

Good or Bad?

O Lord, I will praise thee. Isaiah 12:1

BEGINNING TOGETHER. *Show a knife to the children. Let them tell different uses of a knife. Then say:* Jimmy Brown finds out about some of the bad things that happen with a knife.

LISTENING TOGETHER. "Mommy, Mommy," cried Jimmy from the kitchen. Mrs. Brown heard Jimmy's cries and came running. There in the kitchen stood Jimmy. Blood was running from his hand, and he was crying very hard.

"Jimmy, what happened to you?" asked Mother as she quickly wrapped a bandage around his hand.

"I was cutting this string," sobbed Jimmy. "I wanted to tie it on my truck. But that old knife cut my finger instead."

"There, Jimmy, that takes care of your finger," said Mrs. Brown as she put her arm around him. "You'll have to remember that a knife can be dangerous. It can help me around the kitchen when I cut up the vegetables. But it also can be a bad thing and cause us trouble. A knife can hurt us if we're not careful."

"I'm going to be careful, Mommy. I don't want to get hurt again."

"I hope you don't," smiled Mother. "Do you want to watch me make some cookies?"

"Sure, Mom, that will be fun." Jimmy climbed up on a high stool by the table.

"While you watch maybe you can figure out a riddle. What do you have with you all the time that is good and bad?"

"You said a knife is good and bad. But I never have a knife with me. I can't guess what it is, Mommy. You tell me."

"It's your tongue. Sometimes you are kind when you talk," said Mother.

"But sometimes I say bad things to Betty and Bobby," added Jimmy.

"God knows how we use our tongues. He wants us to use our tongues to say good things. It would be hard to do alone. But our hearts are filled with Jesus' love. Now we want to live a new way. We want to do what God tells us because we love Him. God helps us say kind words. Can you think of the best way to use your tongue, Jimmy?"

"I could tell you that I love you, Mommy," said Jimmy.

"That would be nice, son. But the best way is to tell God how much we love Him. We feel like Isaiah, who wrote: 'O Lord, I will praise Thee.' God forgives us when we sin. He forgives us when we speak unkind words. We want to praise Him for loving us so much."

TALKING TOGETHER. What kind of trouble did Jimmy have? Is a knife always bad? Why did it cause trouble for Jimmy? What part of your body is sometimes used in a good way and sometimes in a bad way? How does God want us to use our tongues? What is one of the best ways to use your tongue?

PRAYING TOGETHER. *Dear God, sometimes I say things that are not kind. I am sorry; forgive me. Help me always to use my tongue to say good things. Use my tongue to tell others of Your love. Amen.*

(Help one of the children say a sentence prayer praising God for His love to us in sending Jesus to be our Savior.)

What Do You Say?

Speak not evil one of another, brethren. James 4:11

BEGINNING TOGETHER. *Ask the family the things they enjoy talking about. Some in the family like to talk about school, others talk about things they see. Then say:* Let's listen to the Brown family and see what they are talking about today.

LISTENING TOGETHER. It is late in the afternoon. Betty came home from school a few minutes ago. She isn't alone, because she invited her friend Debby to play with her for a while. The two girls went down to the basement, where Betty had fixed up a little playroom.

"Let's play house," said Betty.

"No, I don't want to," answered Debby. "We play that all the time. Why don't we play school? You have a blackboard here. And this table could be the desk."

"That's a good idea," agreed Betty. "We could get Jimmy and Janey to be the schoolchildren."

"This sounds like fun," said Debby, laughing a little. "We could take turns being the teacher."

"I'm going to pretend that I am Miss Becker, our teacher at school," suggested Betty. "She's a good teacher."

"Oh, no, I wouldn't ever be Miss Becker; she's too mean," grumbled Debby. "She's always telling us what to do and gets angry. Today she made me stay in and miss recess."

"Debby, Miss Becker isn't mean. Sometimes the children get naughty. She does get angry once in a while, but she's still nice most of the time."

"Betty, how can you say that?" shouted Debby, stamping her foot in anger. "I don't like Miss Becker, and if you want to be like her, I'm not going to play. I'm going home."

"Maybe you can come over tomorrow and play. Good-bye."

Betty followed Debby upstairs and opened the door for her. As Betty turned away from the door, she had a sad look on her face.

Mother looked up from her work. "Betty, it's too bad you and Debby had trouble."

"I don't like Debby to talk that way about Miss Becker," said Betty sadly.

"I was happy to hear the way you talked about your teacher. That is just the way God wants us to talk about others. He would like to remind Debby the way He reminded Christians long ago when He said, 'Speak not evil one of another, brethren.' "

"Does that mean to say good things about other people?" asked Betty.

"Yes, Betty. When our hearts are filled with God's love, we want to say kind things about others."

"I hope God isn't too angry with Debby, Mom."

"God wants to forgive Debby for what she said. I know Debby is probably sorry she said such angry words. She'll think about it and be glad that God wants to forgive her for Jesus' sake."

TALKING TOGETHER. Why did Betty and Debby have an argument? What should Debby have remembered? How does God want us to talk about others? What words of God would be good to think about when we begin talking about others?

PRAYING TOGETHER. *Lord God, I love You and want to do what You want me to do. Help me be kind when I talk about others. Amen.*

(Help one of the children say a sentence prayer asking God to help the brothers and sisters show love to one another in their play.)

God Cares

Cast all your care upon Him, for He careth for you. 1 Peter 5:7

BEGINNING TOGETHER. *Talk briefly about what you do with the family's pets when you go on vacation. Let the children tell why they aren't left alone. Then say:* Mrs. Brown is just getting home with the family from a nice vacation. But she is going to find that she forgot to do something before she left home.

LISTENING TOGETHER. The Browns' short vacation was over. Mr. Brown drove the car up the driveway. As soon as it stopped, Bobby jumped out and ran all around the house. "Oh, it's good to be home. I'm going to run over to see Don for a minute. I'll be right back."

Janey ran to the garage calling, "Here, Taffy! Here, Taffy!" Her little kitten came running, and Janey picked it up. "How are you, Taffy? Are you glad we came home?"

Everyone seemed busy and very happy to be back home. Mr. Brown started unpacking the car. Mrs. Brown went to the kitchen to get supper ready. "It does seem nice to be back home in my own kitchen," she said.

As she was preparing a salad, Betty came running. "Mom, come quick. Something happened to your pretty plant in the living room."

"Oh, oh," said Mrs. Brown as she saw her plant. "I forgot to water it before we left. I'm afraid it's dead. There was no one here to take care of it. Betty, would you check my other plants and see if they need some water?"

"All right, Mommy. I'll do it right away."

It was soon time for supper, and they all came to the table. Each had something new to tell about something he had seen in the few hours they had been home.

Father glanced around the table. "I see that everyone

is finished eating. Tonight, when we talk to God for a few minutes, we should remember a few things about our trip. You know we drove many miles. And every minute of the way God was with us. He watched over us and took care of us."

"I knew He was right there when we were in the storm," interrupted Jimmy.

"And He gave us food to eat," added Janey.

"That's right, children. God loves us, so He does all of this for us. He doesn't want us to worry about anything, so He tells us, 'Cast all your care upon Him, for He careth for you.' We have seen how He takes care of us. He takes care of us so well He sent His Son Jesus to be our Savior. Because of Jesus, we don't worry about anything. We trust in God."

"It's a good thing God doesn't take care of things like Mom took care of her plant," said Bobby with a smile.

"What do you mean, Bobby?"

"Bobby is teasing me a little," laughed Mother. "I forgot to take care of my plant before I left, so it died while we were gone. But you are right, Bobby. God never forgets us. He cares for us every minute no matter if we are at home or maybe at school or on vacation."

TALKING TOGETHER. What had Mother forgotten to do before the trip? Father said they had a special reason to talk with God after their trip. What was it? What are some of the ways in which God takes care of you? What is the most important thing God has done for you?

PRAYING TOGETHER. *Heavenly Father, I thank you for taking care of me. You give me clothes, food, and a home. I thank You, too, for my parents, who love me and watch over me. Most of all I thank You for sending Jesus to be my Savior. Amen.*

(Help one of the children say a sentence prayer asking God to watch over them in their play so no harm comes to them.)

Be Happy

Be happy with what you have.   Hebrews 13:5

BEGINNING TOGETHER. Do you know the story about King Midas? He was such a greedy man that he wanted everything he touched to turn to gold. He wasn't happy with what he had. In the end all the gold didn't make him happy either. In our story today we find that Betty has to learn a lesson about how to be happy.

LISTENING TOGETHER. A new catalog had come in the morning mail. It had pictures of the new clothes for winter. Betty was sitting and looking at the clothes when Mother came in with an armload of coats.

"Well, I'm glad that job is finished. I've been working all morning getting our winter things out. I want you to try on these coats for me. Jimmy, you can be first. Try on this jacket." Jimmy slipped into the coat, but Mother couldn't close it. "Oh-oh, Jimmy, I can't even zip it closed this year. I guess that means a new jacket for you."

"Oh, boy, Mommy! May I have one of those jackets with a fuzzy hood?"

"We'll see, Jimmy. We'll go down to the store and find a nice jacket tomorrow. Betty, I think this was your jacket from last winter. Let's see how it fits. There, that looks fine. I'm glad you'll be able to wear it another year."

"Oh, Mommy, I don't want to wear this old jacket again. I wore it all last year. Jimmy is going to get a new jacket. I want one, too," grumbled Betty.

"Betty, that would be wasteful, to throw this jacket away when it's still good. We can't afford to buy new jackets for everyone each year."

"But I had my new jacket all picked out, Mommy. I don't think it's fair," complained Betty.

"Do you think it's fair to grumble?" asked Mother.

"What do you mean?" asked Betty, looking rather puzzled.

"Where do you think you get your clothes to keep you warm?" asked Mother again.

"Daddy and you buy them at the store," answered Betty.

"But who makes it possible for Daddy to work and earn enough money for your things?"

"I guess God does," said Betty quietly.

"All right, Betty. God has been good to us. He gives us clothes to keep us warm. He gives us a nice home and good food. He does this for us because He loves us. He now asks us to 'be happy with what you have.' "

"I guess I didn't sound very thankful, did I?" said Betty.

"No you didn't, Betty. I know you love God, but you ought to show it also in the way you talk. We have the best reason to be happy because we have Jesus as our Savior. With His love in your heart you can be happy even with an old jacket this year."

"I guess I was jealous of Jimmy. I'm sorry, Mommy. I'll wear my old jacket another year. Next year it will be my turn for a new one."

TALKING TOGETHER. Why did Jimmy need a new jacket? Can you tell why Betty got angry? Who gives you everything you have? What Bible words should you remember when you begin complaining about what you have?

PRAYING TOGETHER. *Heavenly Father, You have given me food and clothes. Thank You for taking care of me. Help me be thankful and not grumble. Amen.*

(Help one of the children say a sentence prayer for the poor people who do not have enough food and clothing.)

Who Made It?

All things were made by Him. John 1:3

BEGINNING TOGETHER. *Let the children tell about some of the pretty things and scenes they remember. Recall together some beautiful scenery found on a trip. Then say:* Do you know how we got our beautiful world? The Brown family is talking about that as we find them today.

LISTENING TOGETHER. It was such a warm evening that the Brown family had stayed out in their yard after dark. Betty and Bobby spread a blanket on the ground and were lying on it looking at the sky.

"I think there are a hundred stars," said Betty.

"There are more than that," answered Bobby. "There are millions, I think. Look at that bright one over there. Isn't it pretty?"

Betty turned a little. "I think I see a crown in the sky. See, those stars look like they are a circle right over us."

"I see the biggest star of all," said Janey.

"Where is it?" asked Jimmy.

"See, it's right over the Martins' house. It's moving a little."

"Oh, no! That's the moon," laughed Bobby.

"It's still pretty," answered Janey.

"You're right, Janey. They are all pretty. Who could tell me how all those beautiful stars and the moon got up there in the sky?" asked Father.

"Don't you know, Daddy?" asked Jimmy.

"Yes, I know, but I wanted to see if you remember."

"God made the stars. I remember because we learned it in Sunday school," said Jimmy.

"God made more than the stars," interrupted Bobby. "He made everything."

"You're both right," agreed Father. "The Bible tells us, 'All things were made by Him.' That means everything in the world and in the sky."

"God must be powerful to do all that," said Betty.

Father turned to Betty. "We learn to know a little about God when we see the beautiful things He made. We see the millions of stars, the trees, plants, and animals. We know He is great and wonderful. Only God could make everything so well."

"He made all this for us to enjoy and to use. God was good to us in creating all this. It makes us want to thank Him and tell Him how good He is," added Mother.

"I want to thank Him for the pretty stars," said Jimmy.

"You can thank Him for everything," replied Father. "You can tell Him anything. Jesus made it possible for you to talk with God."

"I'm going to thank God for Jesus, too," said Bobby.

TALKING TOGETHER. What were the Browns watching one evening? Who made the stars and everything else we see? What should we do when we see God's beautiful world?

PRAYING TOGETHER. *Dear God, You have made a beautiful world for us. Thank You for everything You have given us. Thank You for taking care of us so well that You sent our Savior Jesus. Amen.*

(Help one of the children say a sentence prayer thanking God for some of the blessings He has given the family such as home, food, clothing, and school.)

Growing in Light

I am the Light of the world. John 8:12

BEGINNING TOGETHER. Have you ever left a basket or board on the grass for many days without moving it? What happens to the grass under the board? Have you ever wondered why the grass has turned so yellow and has stopped growing? Maybe we can find out about it from the Brown family today.

LISTENING TOGETHER. It was a beautiful, sunny afternoon. It was so nice, in fact, that Mr. Brown decided to cut the grass before supper. He was working on the mower, putting some oil in the motor. Bobby came out of the house. "Dad, I have a mystery to solve."

"That sounds interesting, Bobby. What is this mystery?"

"Miss Miller, my teacher, had two pretty plants on her desk today. Right before we went home she took one of the plants and put it in a dark closet. She didn't tell us why she did it. She said it was a mystery. We are supposed to find out why she left one plant on her desk and one in the closet. Do you know, Dad?"

"I think so, Bobby. Come over here by the garage. Do you see how green the grass is right here?"

"It looks nice, Dad. But how will this help me solve the mystery?"

"Just a minute and you'll find the answer. Here's a board you forgot to put away last week. Lift it up once."

"Look, Dad, the grass is all yellow and sick looking. Why?" asked Bobby.

"See if you can figure it out. It had plenty of water, and it's nice and warm there in the sun. What's the only thing the grass under the board didn't have?"

"Let's see — it had water and heat, but it was dark under the board. It didn't have any light."

"That's it, Bobby. Plants need light to grow. That is what Miss Miller is trying to show. The plant in the closet will soon turn yellow. If she leaves it there long enough, it will die."

"Light is really very important to us, isn't it, Dad?" said Bobby, thinking carefully.

"Yes, and there's another Light that is the most important of all. Remember that Jesus told us, 'I am the Light of the world.' "

"Dad, I guess Jesus is as important to us as the sunlight is to plants. We can't get along without Jesus, and plants can't get along without light."

"You're right, Bobby. Jesus is our Light because He lived and died for us. He made the darkness of our sins go away. Now our sins are forgiven, and we can live close to God and be happy."

TALKING TOGETHER. What important thing do plants need? Who called Himself "the Light of the world"? Why is Jesus called our Light?

PRAYING TOGETHER. *Lord Jesus, I need You with me every day. Thank You for dying for me to take my sins away. Amen.*

(Help one of the children say a sentence prayer asking God's help to keep the Light of Jesus in our hearts all our lives.)

The Right Size

Let the children come to Me. Mark 10:14

BEGINNING TOGETHER. *Have the children think of occasions when they were told they were too small to do a certain thing. Then say:* Many times you feel you're too little to do anything. In our story you will learn you are the right size for someone who is very important.

LISTENING TOGETHER. Janey heard Bobby and his friends in the backyard, so she ran quickly outside to see if she could play with them. They were getting ready to play ball. "I want Don on my team," said Bobby. "Let's play. You can be up to bat first." Janey ran to the boys. "I want to play, too."

"Go on, Janey, you're too little to play with us." Bobby gave Janey a little shove. "Play with Betty."

Janey was disappointed, but she turned away and went into the house. Betty had brought out her new doll and was changing its clothes. "Betty, may I play with you?"

"Oh, Janey, go play with Jimmy, you're too little. You'll just break my new doll."

Janey turned away again. Now she was sadder than before. "I don't want to play with Jimmy. I'm never the right size," she mumbled. She sat down on the kitchen floor near Mrs. Brown.

"Janey, why do you have your sad face on this morning? You're usually my happy girl."

"Everyone says I'm too little. I can't play with Bobby, and Betty doesn't want me either. I'm just the wrong size for everyone," said Janey sadly.

"You're just the right size for me," smiled Mother.

"You and Daddy might think that, but everyone else says I'm too little," complained Janey.

"You're just the right size for Jesus, and He's the most important of all. One day some mothers brought little children to Jesus. They wanted Jesus to bless them and hold them. But some of Jesus' friends told the mothers to take the children away. They thought Jesus wouldn't want to be bothered with the little children."

"That wasn't very nice. They sound like Bobby and Betty."

"Jesus didn't like it either. He told His friends, 'Let the children come to Me.' He loves children even when they are just like you. He picked up the children in His arms and blessed them. They felt so happy because they were filled with Jesus' love. You are just like those children. So you see, Janey, you are the right size. You can go to Jesus anytime and talk with Him."

"I'm glad Jesus loves me, Mommy."

TALKING TOGETHER. What problem did Janey have one day? Who was the only one who said Janey was not too little? Is anyone too little for Jesus? Tell a Bible story that shows this. How does it make you feel to know that Jesus loves you even though you are not very old?

PRAYING TOGETHER. *Dear Jesus, I am happy that You want children to come to You. Thank You for loving me so much that You died for me. Make my love for You grow stronger every day. Amen.*

(Help one of the children say a sentence prayer thanking God for Sunday school teachers who tell us about Jesus, the Friend and Savior of little children.)

May I Borrow?

The wicked borroweth and payeth not again. Psalm 37:21

BEGINNING TOGETHER. *Talk about things your family has had to borrow from the neighbors. In the discussion bring up the question if it would be all right to keep the borrowed items. Then say:* Listen to the story about the Brown family. They have a problem about borrowing.

LISTENING TOGETHER. Jimmy was playing with his wagon in the driveway. Every time he pulled it, the wagon would squeak very loud.

Jimmy saw his father come out of the garage, so he called to him, "Daddy, could you please fix my wagon?"

"Yes, Jimmy, I think I could fix that for you. We'll have to go over to the Martins to borrow a can of oil." Father and Jimmy went through the gate to the Martins' backyard.

Mr. Martin was working out in the garden. When Mr. Brown told him he needed an oilcan, he said, "Sure, you can borrow one from me. In fact, I think I have two oilcans."

"Thanks, Ken. We'll bring it back when we're finished."

Mr. Brown and Jimmy went back home and began to work on the wagon. "There, that fixes it. Jimmy, will you take the oilcan back to Mr. Martin?"

"Dad, why don't you just put it in our garage? I want to play with my wagon now."

"Jimmy, I promised Mr. Martin to return this oilcan, and that's what we are going to do."

"Don't you think it would be all right to keep it? Mr. Martin said he had two of them, anyway."

"Jimmy!"

"All right, Dad, I'll take it back," grumbled Jimmy. In a few minutes Jimmy was back in his own yard. "I'll help you take those leaves to the backyard if you put them in my wagon, Dad."

"Fine, Jimmy, that would be a big help." Mr. Brown began to load the wagon. "Jimmy, who gave us all the things we have?"

"What do you mean?" asked Jimmy.

"I mean, who has given us our home, our car, our furniture, and everything we call our own?"

"God gave them to us. Everyone knows that."

"Who gave Mr. Martin all the things he has?"

"God did."

"That's right. God has given things to each of us. We are to take care of them for God. And because we love God so much, we also show love to our neighbor. We help him take care of his things too."

"You mean I was wrong before when I wanted to keep that oilcan? But it was just a little thing."

"It may have been small, but it did belong to Mr. Martin. God says, 'The wicked borroweth and payeth not again.' When we love God, we want to do what He tells us. We will help our neighbor keep what belongs to him."

TALKING TOGETHER. What did Mr. Brown borrow from the neighbor? Why did Jimmy want to keep the oilcan? Who has given us everything we have? Why will we also help our neighbor take care of his things?

PRAYING TOGETHER. *Dear God, help me show how much I love You by helping my neighbor. By Your Word remind me to return whatever I borrow. Help me remember that all things belong to You and I am just taking care of them for You. Amen.*

(Help one of the children say a sentence prayer asking God to help them be careful with anything that belongs to a neighbor — his lawns, garden, and home.)

You Are Worth More than a Bird

Fear ye not therefore; ye are of more value than many sparrows.
Matthew 10:31

BEGINNING TOGETHER. *Discuss with the children some of the birds that come into your yard. Then say:* Did you ever see a sparrow? It is such a little bird. They go around chirping in our yards eating little seeds. They are little, but they help teach Jimmy something important.

LISTENING TOGETHER. The sun was warm and the sky was clear one afternoon. Mrs. Brown was busy working in her flowers by the fence. She stopped for a minute and looked around. She thought she had heard someone calling.

Suddenly through the back gate came Jimmy with tears running down his face. He was sobbing so hard he couldn't even talk.

"Jimmy, what's wrong?" Mother put her arms around him. "Now don't cry, son. Everything will be all right."

Slowly Jimmy calmed down and stopped trembling. "Mommy, I am afraid of that dog. It started chasing me, and I was afraid it was going to bite me. Let's go in the house. It might come over here."

"It's too bad you feel afraid, son. The dog won't come here. Sit down beside me."

Jimmy sat down by his mother, but he kept looking over the fence to see if the dog had followed him.

"Jimmy, do you see those little birds flying around my garden?"

"Yes, Mommy, they're just some old sparrows. They're around all the time."

"We have many sparrows in our yard, don't we, son?"

"Sure, so does everyone around here. Bobby says there are millions of sparrows around."

"Jimmy, did you know that God knows and sees each little sparrow? He takes care of each little bird."

"He watches over them all, Mommy?"

"Yes, He knows each of them. See how they fly around. They're not worried about anything."

"I wish I was a bird. Then I could fly high and that dog would never get me."

"Jimmy, I'm trying to tell you that you don't need to be so afraid. God told us, 'Fear ye not therefore; ye are of more value than many sparrows.' God says you are worth more to Him than a sparrow. If He watches over the sparrows so carefully, just think how much more He watches over you. He loves you enough that He sent His own Son, Jesus, to live and die for you."

"You mean I don't have to be afraid of that dog when I go to school tomorrow?"

"No, son. Don't bother about the dog. Just think of these words of God: 'Fear not.' He will watch over you."

TALKING TOGETHER. Why was Jimmy afraid? How did the sparrows help Jimmy see that he shouldn't be afraid? What are some things that make you afraid? Can you think of some words God said that would help you be brave?

PRAYING TOGETHER. *Heavenly Father, sometimes I am afraid. I feel alone and afraid that something will hurt me. Help me remember that You are watching over me. Take away my fear. Amen.*

(Have one of the children add a sentence prayer of his own.)

A Free Gift

The gift of God is eternal life through Jesus Christ, our Lord.
Romans 6:23

BEGINNING TOGETHER. *Let the children tell about some of the things the mailman brings to your house. Help them to recall packages he has delivered. Then say:* In our story today the Brown children are going to get a surprise from the mailman.

LISTENING TOGETHER. For the third time that morning Janey ran to her mother in the kitchen and called, "Is it time yet, Mommy?"

Mother turned to Janey and answered, "Yes, it is finally time for the mailman to be coming."

Janey liked to meet the mailman. She would sit on the front steps every morning waiting for him to come. She sat for a few minutes until finally down the block she saw him walking. She stood up, impatiently jumping on one foot and then the other.

"Do you have any mail for us today?" asked Janey as the mailman came up the front walk.

"Let's see here. Yes, there is a letter for your father and, look here, a surprise for each of the Brown children." The mailman pulled four packages out of his pack.

"Thank you, Mr. Mailman. Mommy, come quick. Look what I got in the mail," cried Janey.

"Let's see, Janey. Oh, that is a package for you from Grandma. You may open it if you like."

Janey eagerly tore off the wrapping paper and opened the gift. "Look, Mommy, it is a book. I like Grandma."

After awhile the rest of the Brown children came home for lunch. "See what Grandma sent us," called Janey the minute they stepped through the door.

The others were soon opening their packages. Each had gotten a new book from Grandma. "Why did she send it to us?" Bobby asked. "It isn't Christmas or anything."

"Grandma just wanted to send you a gift because she loves you," replied Mother.

"I like my new Bible story book. It talks about a gift in here, too."

"What kind of gift is that?" asked Betty.

"It is the most important gift of all," answered Bobby. "It comes from God to us."

"I think Bobby is talking about our new life in heaven. God sent Jesus to forgive our sins. Now with our sins cleaned away we love God and will go to heaven when we die," said Mother.

"I'd like to live in heaven, Mommy. What do we have to do?"

"You can't do anything. God just gives it to you. He loves you so much He wants you to be forgiven and live with Him now, and later in heaven. Jesus made it all possible by suffering and dying for you. We read about it in the Bible: 'The gift of God is eternal life through Jesus Christ, our Lord.'"

"I'm glad we have someone who loves us so much," said Jimmy.

TALKING TOGETHER. What surprise did the Brown children receive in the mail? Why did Grandma send them? What is the most important gift you have received? Why did God do it for you? Who made it possible for you?

PRAYING TOGETHER. *Dear God, thank You for loving me so much that You sent Jesus to live and die for me. It makes me happy to know I will live in heaven someday with You. Be with me here as I live with You every day. Amen.*

(Have one of the children add a sentence prayer of his own.)

Giving Thanks

Oh, give thanks unto the Lord, for He is good. Psalm 106:1

BEGINNING TOGETHER. *Have the family talk about the prayers that are used at mealtime. Then say:* Would you pray if you went to a restaurant to eat? Let's see what the Browns do about this today.

LISTENING TOGETHER. The Brown family was doing something special today because it was Mother's birthday. Father had told everyone to get ready. He wanted to take them out to eat at a restaurant.

"This is going to be fun," said Bobby as the Browns went into the restaurant. A waitress helped them find a table and put menus in front of Mr. and Mrs. Brown.

In a few minutes the Browns ordered what they wanted and then sat back to wait for the food.

"While we're waiting," said Father, "we could say our prayer. Then we'll be ready to eat when the food comes."

"Dad, I didn't see anyone else praying," said Bobby, looking around the room.

"Just because no one else prayed doesn't mean that we'll do the same, Bobby. Do you know why we pray at mealtime?"

"Oh, I guess I do a little."

"When I was a little boy a kind old man told me a story about praying at mealtime that I have always remembered. Would you like to hear it?"

"Sure, Daddy, go ahead," said Betty.

"This old man lived on a farm. He was happy there with his family. One day some friends stopped to see them. The old man invited them to stay for dinner. When everyone sat down at the table, the visitors began to eat right away. The old man stopped them, saying, 'Just a minute! We always say a prayer before we eat.' The visitors replied, 'Go ahead, but we don't believe in doing that.' The old man answered, 'I want to pray before meals. God loves me and has been good to me. He has given me everything I have. I want to thank Him for it.' 'Does everyone on your farm believe like you do?' the visitors asked. 'No, there are a few who don't pray before they eat.' The visitors smiled, 'Who are they?' 'My pigs don't pray before they eat. They just eat. They aren't grateful to have food. They never give thanks.' "

"That was a good story, Dad. I guess I will always remember to pray."

"Remembering a story like that shouldn't be the reason we pray. We pray because we want to thank God. He says: 'Oh, give thanks unto the Lord, for He is good.' God is good to us. He is so good He gave Jesus to forgive and help us. He gives us everything we need to take care of our bodies. That is why we pray."

"Our food does look good. God must love us a lot to give us such good things to eat."

"Let's pray, Dad, so we can eat."

TALKING TOGETHER. Why did the old man in Father's story pray before meals? Who were the only ones on the farm who didn't pray? Where do we get our food? Why should we pray at mealtime?

PRAYING TOGETHER. *Heavenly Father, thank You for giving us food every day. You are so good to us in many ways. Help us remember that all we have comes from You. Amen.*

(Have one of the children add a sentence prayer of his own.)

How Are You Feeling?

Jesus laid His hands upon every one of them and healed them.
Luke 4:40

BEGINNING TOGETHER. *Show the children a fever thermometer. See if they can tell about a time when it was used. Then say:* How did you feel when you were sick? You probably felt as sick as Betty does today.

LISTENING TOGETHER. Mrs. Brown came down the hall carrying a tray of things to Betty's room. As she opened the door, she saw Betty lying on the bed, holding her head.

"Mommy, I feel so sick my head feels like it's going to break."

"I'm sorry you aren't feeling well this morning. Let's take your temperature again." Mrs. Brown put the thermometer in Betty's mouth.

"Mommy," mumbled Betty, trying to talk with the thermometer in her mouth.

"Here, now! You'll have to keep your mouth closed. I talked with Dr. Olson a few minutes ago. If you aren't feeling better tomorrow, he wants to see you. Let's see if your fever is down. No, it looks like it is about the same."

"Mommy, what can we do? I want to get better."

"I know you want to feel better, dear. We have called the doctor. We have kept you in bed. We are giving you medicine. There is one more thing we should do."

"What is that, Mommy?"

"Maybe if I tell you a story, you'll be able to answer that yourself," answered Mother.

"What kind of story are you going to tell?"

"The story I was thinking of is a true story from the Bible. It happened many years ago. People didn't have the good medicines that we have now. Sickness was a terrible thing then, too. The sick people in one little village were happy one day when they heard that a man was preaching to great crowds of people. They heard that this man was able to heal the sick."

"I know who that man was, Mommy. It wasn't just a man. It was Jesus, wasn't it?"

"That's right. They brought many sick people to Jesus. We read in the Bible: 'Jesus laid His hands upon every one of them and healed them.' "

"But, Mommy, how can I go to Jesus so He can make me well?"

"You don't have to go to Jesus. He's right here. All you have to do is talk to Him. He will hear you. Ask Him to make you well. Jesus lived and died to take our sins away. Now we can go to God anytime, and we know He will help us."

"Mommy, I think I feel better already. I'm glad Jesus is ready to help."

TALKING TOGETHER. What was wrong with Betty? What had they done to help her? What was the most important thing to do for her? Jesus heals people when they are not well. What did Jesus do for us to make us new?

PRAYING TOGETHER. *Dear Jesus, there are many people who are feeling very sick. Be with them and heal them if You think it would be best for them. Keep my body strong and healthy so I may live for You. Amen.*

(Have one of the children add a sentence prayer of his own.)

Doers or Hearers?

Be doers of the Word and not hearers only. James 1:22

BEGINNING TOGETHER. *Help the children recall when their grandparents or other relatives were visiting. Talk about something the children did to help them during the visit. Then say:* Today we find that the Browns have a visitor with them.

LISTENING TOGETHER. Grandma Brown had arrived for a little visit with the Brown family. The children were busy showing her around the house.

Finally Grandmother said, "You'll just have to let me sit down for a minute. I'll be here for a week. You'll have time to show me everything."

"I get to sit by Grandma," said Jimmy, wiggling on the sofa.

Janey found a small place on Grandma's lap. "Me, too."

"Now just a minute. Maybe one of you could get my slippers."

"I'll do it," shouted Bobby as he jumped up.

"No, it's my turn to do something," argued Betty as she also ran for the door. The two tumbled over each other and fell down just as Mother came into the room.

"Don't argue, children," said Grandmother. "Betty, you get my slippers. Bobby, maybe you could bring my glasses. They're right in the suitcase, too."

"You can see how glad we all are to have you here, Grandma," laughed Mother.

"I'm glad to be here, too," agreed Grandma.

Bobby and Betty came down the stairs. "Here are your glasses, Grandma, and here are your slippers."

"Thank you, children, that was kind of you."

"We like to do things for you, Grandma," replied Bobby.

Betty jumped up. "Yes, we love you so much we will work all night if you want us to."

Grandma laughed. "I don't think I'll need anything more right now. But you know it's getting late. I imagine it's about time for bed. May I read your Bible story to you tonight?"

"That would be nice. I'll get the book," said Betty.

Grandma read a Bible story to the children. When she was finished, Grandma asked, "You like to hear about God, don't you? But you know it isn't enough just to listen. God says, 'Be doers of the Word and not hearers only.' Bobby, why did you get my glasses when I asked you to do it?"

"I wanted to do it for you, Grandma. I love you."

"That is the same reason we do what God tells us to do. We love Him because He's good to us. He loves us and takes care of us. He loves us so much that He sent Jesus, His own Son, to the world to suffer and die for us. God has forgiven our sins."

"We have many reasons to love Him, don't we?" said Betty quietly.

"Yes, I hope you children will always love Him," added Grandma.

TALKING TOGETHER. Who was visiting the Browns? Why did all the children want to do things for Grandma? Why will we want to do things for God? Can you think of something you could do for God to show Him that you love Him?

PRAYING TOGETHER. *Dear God, fill my heart with the love of Jesus, so that I will gladly do what You say. Amen.*

(Have one of the children add a sentence prayer of his own.)

Are You Ready?

I will come again.   John 14:3

BEGINNING TOGETHER. *Have the family talk about the things they must do to get ready for a trip. Then say:* In our story today someone in the Brown family is busy getting ready for a trip. Let's see what is happening.

LISTENING TOGETHER. "Are you ready?" called Mr. Brown as he stood by the front door.

"We'll be down in a minute," answered Mrs. Brown from upstairs.

"That train won't wait for us if we aren't ready, so hurry. I'll get the car out of the garage."

Grandmother had been visiting the Browns, and now it was time for her to go home. Bobby carried her suitcase down the stairs. "I'll take this out to the car. Are you sure you have everything, Grandma?"

"Yes, Bobby, I'm all ready now," said Grandmother. "Let's go, everyone." Janey, Jimmy, and Betty followed Bobby to the car.

The Browns had to wait a few minutes at the station, but the train finally came in. Grandmother got on the train. As the train slowly pulled out of the station, a man came running with his suitcase. "Wait for me, wait for me," he shouted. But it was too late. He wasn't ready when the train came.

As the Browns drove home Jimmy said, "That man wasn't very happy when he missed his train."

"No," said Father. "But you know, I've been thinking, this reminds me of something that is going to happen when Jesus comes. Jesus told us, 'I will come again.' He wants us to be ready. Many people are going to be like the man at the railroad station. They will not be ready when Jesus comes."

"I'm ready right now for Jesus," said little Janey.

"How do you know if you are ready, Mommy?" asked Jimmy. "Am I ready?"

"Yes, Jimmy," answered Mrs. Brown, "you are ready for Jesus. You love Him and trust Him to take away your sins."

"I'm happy that all the Browns are ready for Jesus to come," smiled Father.

TALKING TOGETHER. Why was Father in a hurry to get to the station? Why didn't the man get on the train? How can you tell if someone is ready for Jesus to come?

PRAYING TOGETHER. *Heavenly Father, I love You. Help me to be ready whenever Jesus comes again. Keep my love for You strong always. Amen.*

(Have one of the children add a sentence prayer of his own.)

A Shepherd

The Lord is my Shepherd. Psalm 23:1

BEGINNING TOGETHER. *Discuss what a shepherd is and does. Have the children recall shepherds they have seen on trips to the West or pictures of shepherds they have found. Then say:* Janey finds out today that a shepherd is also a name used for someone else.

LISTENING TOGETHER. Mr. Brown came in the back door and called, "Hello, is anyone home?" As she sat down in the living room, Mrs. Brown came in with Janey.

"I'm glad you got home a little early. Pastor King will be here in a few minutes. He said he wanted to talk to you."

"That's fine. I was supposed to do some work for him soon."

"Daddy, what does a pastor do?" asked Janey.

"Well, Janey, he is something like a shepherd. He takes care of the people of our church. Maybe I could tell you more later. I think I hear Pastor King at the door."

Pastor King and Mr. Brown talked together for a little while. Janey sat watching them closely. She shook her head slowly and frowned a little. Finally Mr. Brown and the pastor finished their business, and the pastor left.

"Daddy, he isn't a shepherd. He didn't even have a stick like shepherds have."

Mr. Brown smiled a little and gave Janey a hug. "Come here, little girl. I'll try to explain it better."

They sat down together. Mr. Brown said, "I said Pastor King is something like a shepherd. He visits the sick people of the congregation. He watches over and helps all the people of the church."

"Does he do anything for me?"

"Yes, Janey, he makes sure you hear about another shepherd. Do you know who that could be?"

"Do you mean Jesus, Daddy?"

"Yes, Janey. God tells us in the Bible: 'The Lord is my Shepherd.' Jesus watches over us and protects us from all danger just like a shepherd does. A shepherd goes out and finds sheep that get lost. Jesus, our Shepherd, keeps us close to Him, too."

"Daddy, I don't want to get lost from Jesus."

"No, none of us want to be lost. We ask Jesus to make our love for Him stronger so we never go away from Him."

"I want Jesus to hold me very tight."

"I'm sure He will, Janey. He loves you very much. He loved you so much He gave His life for you. He's the Good Shepherd."

TALKING TOGETHER. Who was the special visitor at the Browns' house? Why did Father call him a shepherd? Why is Jesus called our "Good Shepherd"?

PRAYING TOGETHER. *Dear Jesus, thank You for watching over me like a shepherd. I will never be afraid, because I know You love me and are with me. Thank You for giving me a pastor who helps take care of me. Amen.*

(Have one of the children add a sentence prayer of his own.)

The Best Gift

Thanks be to God for His unspeakable gift. 2 Corinthians 9:15

BEGINNING TOGETHER. *Have a small birthday candle, and ask the children what they think of when they see the candle. Then say:* Can you remember your last birthday? What are some of the things that happened on your birthday? There is a birthday in the Brown house as we find them today.

LISTENING TOGETHER. There is the sound of happy singing in the dining room at the Browns' home. Betty is having a birthday. She is certainly a happy girl. Mother has just brought the birthday cake to the table, and the entire family sings to Betty.

While Mother cuts the cake, Bobby and Jimmy run to the other room. They bring back some brightly wrapped packages.

"What's in this big one?" said Betty excitedly.

"I guess you'll have to open it to see," suggested Mother.

"Look, everyone! It's a new doll. Oh, thank you, Daddy! It's just what I wanted."

"Open this one next." Jimmy pointed to a long, pink package. "That's the one I got for you."

"Jimmy, you look as excited as Betty," teased Mother.

Betty opened the package. "Thank you, Jimmy. This coloring book is so nice. I needed a new one. Oh, thank you, everyone. My birthday is a very happy birthday."

"Since we have all the cake eaten and the gifts opened, it is time to talk just a few minutes about the best gift Betty received," said Father.

"I know, we'll talk about her new doll," replied Bobby.

"No, we won't. We'll talk about the coloring book I gave her," argued Jimmy.

"I'm afraid you're both wrong. The gift I'm thinking about is a gift that Betty has every day."

"I know! It's a gift from God," said Bobby.

"Now you're right, Bobby," said Father. "God sent Jesus. He's your best gift. Jesus came, and now you have a new life. Your sins are forgiven. You have Jesus' love in your heart."

"That's my best gift," smiled Betty. "God loves me. That gift won't get old like this doll."

"No, and it won't wear out like that coloring book," said Mother. "This is a gift you want to share with everyone."

"Betty, you thanked each of us for the gifts we gave you. Do you want to thank anyone else for a gift?"

"Yes, Daddy, let's thank God for His best gift of Jesus."

"That's a good idea. God told Paul to write some words in the Bible about this. He said: 'Thanks be to God for His unspeakable gift.' That's what we want to say, too."

TALKING TOGETHER. What special day was it in the Browns' home? What was Betty's best gift? Why is this your best gift, too? What will we want to do now that we know about this wonderful gift?

PRAYING TOGETHER. *Dear God, I am always happy to receive a gift. Your gift of forgiving my sins is the best of all. Thank You for sending Jesus so I could be forgiven. Help me share this gift with others. Amen.*

(Have one of the children add a sentence prayer of his own.)

Whom Do You Love the Most?

Thou shalt love the Lord thy God with all thy heart.
Matthew 22:37

BEGINNING TOGETHER. *Talk about some of the people each of the family loves. Bring out in the discussion that we love some people more than others. Then say:* We show whom we love the most by what we do. Bobby Brown didn't understand this at first. But he finally knew what it meant, as we see in our story today.

LISTENING TOGETHER. Mr. Brown was busy writing a letter when Bobby came running through the door. "Dad! Dad! Where are you?"

"I'm in the living room, Bobby. Take it easy. I won't run away."

"Don and his family are going to take their boat up to the lake tomorrow. They asked me to go along. May I go with them, Dad? We'll be going fishing and take a ride in the boat and have a picnic and —"

"Hold on there, Bobby. Just one thing at a time," said Mr. Brown. "Now just who invited you to go along?"

"Well, Don was telling me about this trip they were taking. Then he said he wanted me to come along. So he asked his mother, and she said they would have plenty of room. So may I go, please?"

"What day is tomorrow, Bobby?" asked Father.

"Let's see. Tomorrow is Sunday. But what has that got to do with it?"

"Are Don and his family going to church first?"

"No, they want to get started early before the lake gets too crowded."

"Do you think you'd want to do it?"

The smile went from Bobby's face. "I know I should go to church, but, Dad, I want to go to the lake, too."

"It would be easy for me to tell you to just go up to the lake and have a good time. But I think it would be best for you to figure out what would be best."

"How can I figure out what to do?"

"A good place to begin is to go to God Himself. He says, 'Thou shalt love the Lord thy God with all thy heart.' "

"I do love Him with my whole heart, Dad."

"Ask yourself, 'If I go to the lake and miss church, would I be showing how much I love God? Would I show that I am thankful for the love of my Savior Jesus?' "

Bobby sat quietly for a few minutes. Mr. Brown began to write his letter again. Suddenly Bobby got up and started on his way outside. Mr. Brown called after him, "Did you decide what you would do, Bobby?"

"I can't go with Don tomorrow. It just wouldn't be much fun. I would be thinking all the time that I was missing church."

"Bobby, I'm happy you feel that way. I'll tell you what we'll do. We'll ask Mother to pack a picnic lunch. Tomorrow after church we'll go over to the park."

"That sounds like a lot of fun, Dad. See you later."

TALKING TOGETHER. What problem did Bobby have? Where did Bobby find the answer to his problem? Can you think of some times when you can show that you love God with your whole heart?

PRAYING TOGETHER. *Heavenly Father, be with me. Give me Jesus' love so I can love You more than anything else. Thank You for church and Sunday school. Amen.*

(Have one of the children add a sentence prayer of his own.)

Guess Who

O Lord, You have searched me and known me. Psalm 139:1

BEGINNING TOGETHER. *Let the children talk about dressing up in costumes on Halloween. Then say:* In our story today it isn't Halloween, but Jimmy is trying to fool some-one. Let's see if he is able to do it.

LISTENING TOGETHER. Jimmy had been busy playing in his room all afternoon. He had been looking through a box of old toys in the closet. 'Way at the bottom of the box he found an old mask from Halloween. He put it on and looked into the mirror.

"I do look like a clown," said Jimmy to himself. "Maybe I could fool Mommy." He found an old shirt of Bobby's and a patched-up pair of pants. Then he went quietly out-side and ran around to the front door.

Mother came to the door, and Jimmy said in his deepest voice, "Hello, lady, could you give me some cookies?"

"Oh, Jimmy, you look funny. Of course, come in and we'll see if there are any cookies in the cookie jar."

Jimmy took off his mask, but there wasn't a happy face under it. "How did you know it was I, Mommy? I thought I could fool you." He looked very disappointed.

"Jimmy, I know you too well to be fooled. I know how you walk and how you talk. I know everything about you."

"I fooled Mr. Martin when I was outside. I was coming down the driveway to go to the front door. Mr. Martin came out of his garage and asked me what I was doing in the Browns' yard. He didn't know who I was until I took off my mask."

"See, Jimmy, you can fool someone. You probably could fool Janey, too. But it is hard to hide from someone who knows you well."

In a few minutes Jimmy was sitting in the kitchen eating some cookies. "I know someone else I couldn't fool, Mommy. Do you know who that is?"

"Let me see." Mother thought a minute. "I think you would have a hard time fooling your Daddy."

"No, I didn't mean him. Guess again," smiled Jimmy.

"I just can't think of anyone else," answered Mother.

"I know I couldn't fool God, because He knows me best of all."

"You are right, Jimmy. In the Bible we read just what you have been saying. It begins: 'O Lord, You have searched me and known me.' Then the writer David tells that God sees us when we are walking or lying down resting. He knows what words we say. He sees us in the darkness and in the light. He knows about us all the time."

"I'm glad God can see me all the time. I don't have to be afraid, but —"

"But what, Jimmy? What's the matter?" asked Mother.

"If God sees me all the time, He sees me when I'm bad, too." Jimmy frowned a little.

"That's right, Jimmy. But that is what makes God's love for us so important. God wants to forgive the bad things we do. We don't have to be afraid of God. We can love Him because He loves us. We know He loves us. He gave His own Son Jesus for us."

"I'm glad God sees me," smiled Jimmy.

TALKING TOGETHER. Did Jimmy fool anyone with his mask? Why couldn't he fool Mother? Can we hide from God? When can God see you? Do you have to be afraid of God? Why not?

PRAYING TOGETHER. *Dear God, You know I am bad some-times, because You see everything I do. Forgive me when I don't do what You want me to do. Amen.*

(Have one of the children add a sentence prayer of his own.)

Who Never Sleeps?

He that keepeth thee will not slumber. Psalm 121:3

BEGINNING TOGETHER. *Place a small alarm clock where the children can see it. Move the hands to show their bedtime. Show the hours they sleep. Then say:* While you are sleeping, other people are wide awake. In our visit with the Browns today we find out about some people who stay awake when you are asleep.

LISTENING TOGETHER. Mr. and Mrs. Brown were getting ready to go to bed. The children had been sleeping for several hours. Mr. Brown checked the doors, and Mrs. Brown made certain the children were covered.

Mr. Brown stood looking out the front window. "Look! Doesn't it look like a fire down in the next block?"

Mrs. Brown came over to the window and looked out. "You're right! I think I hear the fire engines coming. I hope the children don't wake up."

The fire trucks went right past the house with their sirens going very loud. Soon other cars and several police cars went past.

"I think I'll go down to see if they need any help," said Mr. Brown as he put on his coat.

As he closed the door behind him, Mrs. Brown heard a noise on the stairs. She turned and there was Bobby rubbing his eyes.

"What's going on around here?" asked Bobby. "I thought I heard a fire engine."

"You did, Bobby. There's a fire down in the next block. Daddy went down to see if he could help."

Mrs. Brown and Bobby waited some time, and finally Mr. Brown came home.

"Everything's fine. It was just dry grass and weeds

burning in a vacant lot. The firemen got there in time to stop it from getting to anyone's home."

"Dad, how could the firemen get here so quick?"

"Bobby, someone is always awake at the fire station to answer any calls that come in."

"You mean they stay awake all night?"

"Yes, some of them do. Others sleep at the station and can be ready in a minute to jump into the trucks."

"That makes me feel good, to know someone is awake and watching," said Bobby.

"That is about how David felt, Bobby. He wrote in a beautiful psalm in the Bible: 'He that keepeth thee will not slumber.' He was talking about God. He meant that God is watching over us every minute."

"That's a lot better than having a fireman watching. Now I really feel safe. God will watch over all of us when even you and Mommy are asleep. God will never go to sleep."

"It makes us happy to know that God loves us so much He takes such good care of us. He loved us enough to send Jesus as our Savior."

"I'm tired, Dad. I can go upstairs alone. I know God is right with me."

TALKING TOGETHER. What awoke Bobby one night? How were the firemen able to get there so quickly? Who is it that watches over us every minute of the day and night?

PRAYING TOGETHER. *Dear God, I feel safe knowing You are watching over me all the time. Keep all my family in Your loving care. Amen.*

(Have each member of the family add a sentence prayer based on needs of the family and others.)

God Made Me

I am fearfully and wonderfully made. Psalm 139:14

BEGINNING TOGETHER. Look at your hand. See how wonderfully God made it. What are some of the ways you use your hands? We sometimes forget how much we use our hands and the other parts of our body. Sometimes we must see a person like Janey did one afternoon before we remember these wonderful gifts.

LISTENING TOGETHER. This was Janey's favorite afternoon. Every week Janey and Mother would go shopping. Janey liked to ride in the grocery cart at the supermarket. As they went along Janey was asking one question after another.

Finally Mother said, "Janey, you're going to have to be quiet so I can get my shopping finished."

Janey was quiet for a few minutes, but soon she leaned over and was pulling on Mother's sleeve, "Mommy, Mommy," she whispered softly.

"What is it now, Janey?"

"Why does that man have only one leg?" Janey pointed to a man ahead of them in the aisle. "Did God make him that way?"

"That man probably lost his leg in an accident, Janey."

"Can he run like me?"

"No, there are many things that man isn't able to do with only one leg."

"I'm sure glad I can run," said Janey. "Can I tell Daddy about the man when we get home?"

"Yes, Janey, you may tell Daddy, but right now you can help me by being very quiet. We're almost finished."

In a few more minutes Mother and Janey were on their way home. They put away the groceries and soon had supper started.

When Mr. Brown came home, Janey rushed out to meet him. "Daddy, you know what I saw at the store?"

"No, I can't imagine what it could be. Was it something nice?" asked Mr. Brown.

"No, it was something sad, Daddy. We saw a man who had only one leg. He couldn't even run."

"That *is* too bad," replied Mr. Brown. "Did you ever think how happy you should be that you have two good legs?"

"I just run around. I never thought about my legs."

"Janey, you have eyes to see God's beautiful world. You have hands that are made so well to do many things. You have ears to hear God's birds sing. You have a voice with which to talk. Once a great man named David wrote a song about it in the Bible. He thought about how God had made him, and he said, 'I am fearfully and wonderfully made.' We have a wonderful body but it was also filled with sin. God sent Jesus, His Son, to live and die for us. Because of Jesus He forgives our sins."

"God is good to me, isn't He, Daddy?" asked Janey.

"Yes, He is good to us. Now we can use our body to thank and love Him. We can use our voice to praise Him. We can use our ears to hear His Word. We want to do this because our hearts are filled with God's love."

TALKING TOGETHER. What did Janey see in the store that bothered her a little? Can you think of something you should do because you have a healthy body? Talk about some ways you can use your body to show how thankful you are to have it.

PRAYING TOGETHER. *Heavenly Father, You have given me a wonderful body. Thank You for giving it to me and making it new because of Jesus. Help me to use my body to love You. Amen.*

(Have each member of the family add a sentence prayer based on needs of the family and others.)

Lights Out

Thy Word is a lamp unto my feet and a light unto my path.
Psalm 119:105

 Put a burned-out light bulb in a lamp. Show the children what happens when you try to use the lamp. Then say: Today a burned-out light bulb gives Mr. Brown some trouble.

 Mr. Brown had just finished tucking Janey in bed. He listened while she prayed. Then he kissed her good-night and turned off the light. He went out of the door to go to Jimmy's room. Suddenly there was a big crash. Mr. Brown fell on the floor.

The crash brought all the children out of their beds, and Mrs. Brown came running up the stairs. "What happened, Daddy?" asked Bobby. "Are you hurt?"

Mr. Brown slowly got to his feet and limped over to the stairs and sat down. "I guess I'm all right. My leg hurts a little."

"My, the way it sounded, I thought you would have a broken leg." Mrs. Brown sat down on the stairs, too. "How did you fall?"

"That light is burned out in the hallway, and I didn't see that chair standing there. So, bang, that's about it."

"I'm going to get a light put in there right away. I'm not even going to wait until morning," said Mrs. Brown. "We don't want anyone else to go stumbling around in the dark."

"Daddy, I forgot to study my Bible verse for Sunday school. Would you help me with it?" asked Bobby.

"All right, Bobby, you jump into bed and I'll help you." Mr. Brown followed Bobby to his room.

"I know part of the verse already, Dad. But the last part I always get mixed up."

"Read your verse, Bobby."

" 'Thy Word is a lamp unto my feet and a light unto my path.' "

"That is an important part of God's Word to know. It draws a beautiful picture for us and helps us to understand it better."

"What do you mean by a picture, Dad?"

"When you think about it, you can see a man walking along a dark place. He can see where he is going because of a light. The man needs the light because otherwise he might stumble and fall."

"That almost sounds like you out in the hall tonight, Dad," smiled Bobby.

"That's right, Bobby. God is telling us that we need His Word to light the way to Him and to heaven. Without God's Word we couldn't see God, and we couldn't see Jesus, the Way. The light of His Word shows us that God loves us. Now every day we can walk with God knowing He has taken away the darkness."

TALKING TOGETHER. Why did Father fall? Can you tell why God's Word is like a light for us? Why do we need the light of God's Word?

PRAYING TOGETHER. *Dear God, thank You for giving us the Bible so we could learn about You. Now we know that You love us and sent Jesus. Stay with me so I may always keep Your love in my heart. Amen.*

(Have each member of the family add a sentence prayer based on needs of the family and others.)

Hands Off!

You shall not steal. Exodus 20:15

BEGINNING TOGETHER. *If you have made a trip to the mountains or have a picture of the mountains, talk about it with your family. Then say:* Today one of the little mountain animals brings some trouble to Bobby.

LISTENING TOGETHER. The Browns had come on a trip to the mountains. They were staying with some friends in a cabin. Even though it was early in the morning, Betty and Bobby jumped out of bed so they could hike down to the lake.

"Betty, did you see my little whistle? I left it right on the dresser."

"No, I saw it there when we went to bed. Did you look all around?"

"It just isn't here. All that's on the dresser is this tiny pine cone."

"Dad told me to take my whistle with me if we went down to the lake this morning. If we have any trouble, we're supposed to blow it. Then they can find us. But now we can't go."

Betty and Bobby sat down looking rather gloomy and wondering what to do. Just then their father came in from the woodpile with an armload of wood.

"What's the trouble? Everyone should look happy on a bright morning like this."

"My whistle is gone, Dad. All that's left is a pine cone. Did you take it?"

Father laughed a little. "No, but I think I know what happened to it. Mr. Daniels told me they were having trouble with some little animals called pack rats. They come into the cabin and take bright, shiny things. They always leave behind something in its place. Come along,

Bobby, I'll show you where they have their nest." In a few minutes Mr. Brown and Bobby found the pack rat's nest. There they found Bobby's whistle.

"I guess animals don't know about stealing, do they, Dad?" said Bobby.

"No, they don't know anything about God's Law that tells us: 'You shall not steal.' But we know about it."

"I never steal," boasted Bobby.

"You sound very sure of yourself, Bobby. I'm glad God's love is in your heart and you want to do what He says. But all of us are tempted to take things that don't belong to us. Remember when Don lost a nickel and you found it and didn't return it? That was stealing."

"I guess I did steal. I didn't have a nickel, so I kept his."

"We can be happy with the things God has given us. We are happiest because He gave His own Son to be our Savior. He forgives us when we do something like you did when you kept Don's nickel. When we are filled with Jesus' love we want to obey God."

TALKING TOGETHER. How did Bobby's whistle disappear? What does God say about taking things that belong to someone else?

PRAYING TOGETHER. *Dear God, help me to be happy with what I have. Forgive me if I have kept something that was not mine. Give me more of Jesus' love that I will want to obey You. Amen.*

(Have each member of the family add a sentence prayer based on needs of the family and others.)

What Is Inside?

The Lord looketh on the heart. 1 Samuel 16:7

BEGINNING TOGETHER. *Let the children look at and hold a plastic flower. Talk about it, bringing out that it looks very natural but when you touch it you can tell it isn't real. Then say:* Today Janey Brown learns about things that look good but are not real.

LISTENING TOGETHER. Mrs. Brown finished dusting the fruit bowl on the kitchen table and went on with her work in the living room. Bobby looked at the fruit. It looked real, but it was made of plastic. Bobby wondered why his mother liked to have it for a decoration. He would have liked to have real fruit in the bowl so he could eat some.

As he looked at the fruit, he got an idea. He began to smile and called to Betty. "I have an idea, Betty. Let's play a trick on Janey."

"What are you going to do, Bobby?" asked Betty.

"See this plastic fruit? Let's try to fool Janey," laughed Bobby. "Janey, Janey, where are you? I have something for you."

Janey came running. "What do you have, Bobby?"

"Here, Janey," said Bobby, "I have this nice apple for you."

"Thank you, Bobby." Janey smiled as she took the apple. She took a big bite and then looked at Bobby with a frown on her face.

Betty and Bobby began to laugh. "We sure fooled you. You thought that was a real apple, didn't you?"

"I don't think you're nice, Bobby," cried Janey.

Just then Mother walked into the kitchen. "What's going on out here, children?"

"We were just teasing Janey a little."

"Do you think that was very kind, children?" asked Mother.

"Well —" mumbled Bobby.

"I think you know it was wrong. Janey, this is a plastic apple. It looks good, but there's nothing inside."

"I wanted to eat it," said Janey sadly.

"You can't eat it, but this apple can help us learn something."

Bobby frowned. "What can an old apple teach me?" he asked.

"It looks very good on the outside. It's just like many people. They may seem very nice, but being nice is not enough. The Bible tells us: 'The Lord looketh on the heart.'"

"I know what that means," interrupted Betty. "We can't fool God. He looks right into our hearts. He can tell if we really love Him."

"Yes, Betty. God can tell if the love of Jesus fills our hearts. Some people think they can fool God. They believe they can pretend to love Him. But God knows if we really trust in Him."

TALKING TOGETHER. How did Bobby and Betty fool Janey? What lesson did the plastic apple teach the children? Why can't we ever fool God? What would God see if He looked into your heart?

PRAYING TOGETHER. *Heavenly Father, I know You look into my heart. You know that I love You. Give me the love of Jesus so there is no room left for sin. Amen.*

(Have each member of the family add a sentence prayer based on needs of the family and others.)

A Warm Gift

Trust in the Lord and do good. Psalm 37:3

BEGINNING TOGETHER. Can you imagine boys and girls walking around barefoot in the snow? That is what happens in some countries where they do not have enough clothing. Some people have to wear what we call rags — clothes so full of holes they hardly hang together. Today Betty and Janey find out more about helping these people.

LISTENING TOGETHER. The sounds of busy people had been coming from the bedrooms all morning. Mother was cleaning out the closets, and she had two good helpers, Betty and Janey.

"Here, Betty, this is the last of the clothes to go into that box," said Mother, handing Betty an old coat.

"Why are you packing all those things in the box, Mother?" she asked.

"These are going to be warm gifts for people in other countries," answered Mother.

"What do you mean by warm gifts?" asked Betty.

Before Mother had a chance to answer, Janey stumbled over the rug and fell right into the big box of clothes.

"Is that what you mean by a warm gift, Mother?" laughed Betty.

"No, that isn't what I had in mind, although Janey would be a nice gift for anyone. I was thinking about people who don't have enough clothes to wear."

"Doesn't everyone have something to wear like we have, Mother?"

"No. It is sad, but in some countries people have so few clothes that the children have to take turns wearing the coats and shoes to go outside. The others have to stay in bed to keep warm."

"I see what you mean by a warm gift now. These coats will keep them warm when it is cold," said Betty. "But why do we have to do it, Mommy? Couldn't someone else take care of them?"

"We send these clothes down to the church. There they will be packed up and sent on a ship over the ocean. We are doing it because we love God. When we love Him, we show our love to others who are in need. He tells us: 'Trust in the Lord and do good.' God has been good to us in so many ways. Can you think of one way God has been good to us, Janey?"

"I have nice clothes to wear. And you are going to give us something to eat for lunch."

"I know something that is most important of all," said Betty. "God sent His Son Jesus to suffer and die for us."

"That does show how good God has been to us. He wants to forgive us. We have seen how much God loves us. Now we want to do good things for others. We want to 'trust in the Lord and do good.' "

TALKING TOGETHER. What was the warm gift Mother was gathering? Can you tell why the Browns were gathering the clothes? Why would we want to help others who need food or clothes?

PRAYING TOGETHER. *Dear Lord, thank You for giving me clothes to keep me warm. Fill my heart with Your love that I also want to help others. Help me remember that all I have comes from you. Amen.*

(Have each member of the family add a sentence prayer based on needs of the family and others.)

No Door

I am the Door. John 10:9

BEGINNING TOGETHER. How do you get into the house? How do you get into the school? How do you get into church? Each answer is the same. You must go through a door. The answer is easy because everyone knows how a door must be used. In our story about the Browns we find that they are looking for a door.

LISTENING TOGETHER. This was a special day at the Brown house. Father had promised the children he would build a playhouse for them in the backyard. Today was his day off, so the Browns had been busy all morning.

"Jimmy, could you hand me that board, please?" Mr. Brown took the board from him and put it in place.

"Daddy, when can we play in it?"

"I think you could play in it in a few minutes. It's almost finished except for painting."

"Hurry, Daddy, I can't wait." Betty jumped up and down in excitement.

"There, I guess that's the last nail," said Mr. Brown.

"May we go in now, Daddy?"

"Go right ahead. Maybe Mommy will bring your lunch out here for you. Would you like that?"

"That'll be fun, Daddy." Bobby looked all around the playhouse. "How do we get in?"

"Just go through the door," answered Father.

"But where is it? There's no door here in the front."

"It must be on the other side." Mr. Brown walked to the other side.

"No, Dad, there isn't any door over here," called Bobby.

"Oh, no!" said Father. "I think we put some boards over the door. You can't even get into your playhouse."

"What are we going to do, Daddy?" asked Janey, looking very sad.

"We'll just make a door. Here, pull off several boards, and then you'll be able to get in."

Mr. Brown pulled off several boards, and there was a nice little door. The children went into their playhouse.

"Have fun, children. I'll see if Mommy has some lunch fixed."

In a few minutes Mr. Brown came out with some sandwiches and fruit. "Here's something to eat. Do you have a place to put it down?"

"Put it here, Dad. Should we pray out here?"

"Why not, Betty? We can talk to God from any place. We can come to Him anytime. Jesus made that possible. Only through Jesus can we come to God."

"Jesus is something like a door, isn't He, Daddy?"

"Yes, in fact Jesus uses those very words. He said, 'I am the Door.' Jesus is the only way to get to God. Jesus suffered and died for us. Now we can go to God and not be afraid. We know God loves us and forgives us for Jesus' sake."

TALKING TOGETHER. What was wrong with the new playhouse? Who is the "door" to God? How did Jesus make a door to God for us?

PRAYING TOGETHER. *Lord Jesus, I do many wrong things every day. I am sorry for them. Forgive me, and give me Your love to forgive others. Amen.*

(Have each member of the family add a sentence prayer based on needs of the family and others.)

Busy Signal

Call upon Me in the day of trouble. Psalm 50:15

BEGINNING TOGETHER. *Talk about using the telephone. Let the children tell about times they spoke over the telephone. Then say:* It is very helpful to have a telephone in your home. But do you know that you have something better than a telephone with which you can talk to someone? Our visit with the Browns will help give you the answer.

LISTENING TOGETHER. Janey Brown was a small girl, but she tried to be a very big girl. The other Brown children were at school this morning. Mother was mixing a batch of cookies. Of course, Janey was right there helping.

Janey got very thirsty. She thought she would show her mother how big she was and get a drink by herself. She climbed up by the kitchen sink and reached for a glass. But poor Janey was not as big as she thought she was. She slipped and landed with a big crash on the floor.

Mrs. Brown ran to Janey and picked her up. Janey's arm had been cut by the broken glass. Janey cried as she saw the blood running down her arm. Mrs. Brown quickly wrapped a clean towel around her arm. "Janey, we'll have to call Dr. Olson to take a look at this arm. But first I want to call Daddy and let him know what happened. If he's not too busy, he might meet us at the doctor's office."

Mrs. Brown went quickly to the phone and tried to get Mr. Brown. But when she dialed the number, she got a busy signal. She couldn't get Mr. Brown. After a minute she tried again, but again there was a busy signal.

"We'll have to go alone, Janey. I can't get Daddy."

Janey and Mrs. Brown hurried to the doctor. He took care of Janey's arm and bandaged it for her. When Janey and Mother came home, Janey lay down to rest.

At lunch everyone was asking questions about Janey's arm. "I'm sure glad Janey's all right," said Jimmy.

"We are all happy she wasn't hurt too badly," added Mr. Brown. "That could have been a serious accident. I just wish I could have been there with you. I'm sorry the phone was busy."

"This would be a good time to thank God for being with Janey. You know, it's a good thing that talking to God is not like talking on a telephone. God is never too busy to hear us," said Mother.

"Mother is right, children," agreed Mr. Brown. "God tells us: 'Call upon Me in the day of trouble.' He wants us to talk with Him because He loves us. We are His children, and He is our heavenly Father. We talk to Him just like you talk to me."

"How did we get to be God's children?" asked Jimmy.

"Jesus made us God's children. He took away our sins and brought us back to God's family. Now we belong to Him."

TALKING TOGETHER. How did Janey get hurt? Why wasn't Father with Janey when she went to the doctor? Is God ever too busy to listen to us? What words of God show us that God wants us to talk to Him? What are some things we would want to tell God?

PRAYING TOGETHER. *Dear God, I am happy that Jesus made me a part of Your family so I can talk to You anytime. I know You are never too busy to listen. Thank You for answering my prayers. Amen.*

(Have each member of the family add a sentence prayer based on needs of the family and others.)

Angel Guards

He shall give His angels charge over thee. Psalm 91:11

BEGINNING TOGETHER. Can you think of some things that are dangerous for children to do? Playing with fire is one. What are some other things that are dangerous? Jimmy has many things to learn about danger. Let's see the trouble that Jimmy is having today.

LISTENING TOGETHER. Jimmy was very proud because he was playing ball with the big boys. Usually the big boys told Jimmy to go away, but today they needed another player, so they told Jimmy he could play in the outfield.

Don was up to bat. Bobby pitched a very fast ball, and Don swung as hard as he could but missed the pitch. Bobby laughed a little at him and shouted, "What's the matter? Didn't you see the ball?"

Don didn't say anything. He just waited for Bobby to pitch. This time Don didn't miss. He hit the ball very hard. It went so far that it went over Jimmy's head and bounced right into the street.

Jimmy knew he didn't want Don to get a home run. He wanted the other boys to think he was very big, so Jimmy went running right out into the street after the ball.

"Jimmy, look out!" shouted Bobby. A car was coming very fast down the street.

When the driver saw Jimmy run out in front of him, he stepped on his brakes as fast as he could. The tires screeched as the car skidded along the street. Jimmy stopped in the middle of the street. He saw the car, but he was so frightened he couldn't move.

Everyone stopped and watched. The car finally came to a stop. It stood there just a few inches from Jimmy.

The boys all ran over to see how Jimmy was. "Are you all right, Jimmy?" asked Bobby.

"I think I'm all right." But he was so frightened he began to cry.

Mr. Brown had heard the noise and came running from the backyard. He picked up Jimmy in his arms and talked quietly to him. When he found that Jimmy wasn't hurt, everyone went over to the Browns front porch and sat down. No one felt like playing ball anymore.

"Jimmy, I know I don't have to tell you that you did something wrong. You can be very happy you had someone guarding you out there in the street."

"I didn't see anyone," sobbed Jimmy. "I was alone with that big car, and it almost hit me."

"You weren't alone, Jimmy. God sent His angels to take care of you. He promised that in a beautiful song in the Bible: 'He shall give His angels charge over thee.' They watch over us and keep us from harm."

"Why does God send His angels, Daddy?"

"God does it because He loves us and wants to take care of us. It is the same reason He gives us all the other things we have. It is the same reason He sent Jesus to be our Savior."

TALKING TOGETHER. What happened to Jimmy while he was playing ball? Why wasn't Jimmy hurt? Who watches over you? Can you think about times of danger when the angels must help you?

PRAYING TOGETHER. *Heavenly Father, I do not have to be afraid, because I know You send Your angels to watch over me. Keep harm and danger away from me. Amen.*

(Have each member of the family add a sentence prayer based on needs of the family and others.)

Let's Sing

Oh, come, let us sing unto the Lord. Psalm 95:1

BEGINNING TOGETHER. What are some of your favorite songs? Do you know some songs about God? What is your favorite song about God? The Brown family likes to sing. As we listen to our story today, maybe we can find out their favorite song.

LISTENING TOGETHER. It was almost time for bed. Janey was the first one to be finished with her bath, so she had come downstairs to the living room. She sat down at the piano and began to sing. She was pretending to play the song on the piano. But, of course, it didn't sound much like a song, because Janey really couldn't play.

Bobby came down the stairs quietly and stood grinning by the door.

Mrs. Brown finally came into the room and asked, "What are you doing here?"

"I was just watching Janey trying to play the piano. That was so funny," laughed Bobby.

"I don't think it's funny. Janey was singing to Jesus, and I'm sure He thought it was fine. He liked it because it came from a little heart filled with love for Him."

"I was just teasing a little, Mom. Why don't we all sing a few hymns before we go to bed? I'll get Dad and Betty and Jimmy."

"That's a good idea, Bobby. Come, everyone," called Mother.

The Brown family was soon gathered around the piano. Mother played some hymns while the rest of the family sang. While they were singing, Father noticed that Jimmy got very quiet.

"What's the matter, son?" asked Father.

"Oh, nothing. I was just wondering why we sing," answered Jimmy.

"I know," said Betty. "We sing because we love God."

"Betty is right. When we sing we can tell God how much we love Him. We can say we are sorry we sin. We can tell Him how thankful we are to Him for sending Jesus to suffer and die for us. It is a wonderful way to worship God."

"But do you think God really likes it?" asked Jimmy.

Father nodded his head. "I'm sure God likes to hear you sing. Many times in His Word He talks about people singing to Him. We all feel like David, who wrote in a psalm, 'Oh, come, let us sing unto the Lord.'"

"It's almost time for bed," said Mother. "Janey, do you want to choose the last song?"

"Mommy, could we sing about the lost light?" asked Janey.

"I think Janey means 'Now the Light Has Gone Away.' That would be a good song to sing before we go to bed."

Now the light has gone away;
Father, listen while I pray,
Asking Thee to watch and keep
And to send me quiet sleep.

Jesus, Savior, wash away
All that has been wrong today;
Help me every day to be
Good and gentle, more like Thee.

TALKING TOGETHER. How did the Browns worship God one night? What are some of the things we can tell God when we sing? How do we know that God really wants us to sing to Him?

PRAYING TOGETHER. *Dear God, I want to thank and praise You for being good to me. Fill my heart every day with the*

(Have each member of the family add a sentence prayer based on needs of the family and others.)

DATE DUE